# Outdoor Maintenance & Repairs

Published by Sharon Publications
Distributed by Sharon Marketing
Fort Lee, New Jersey
Under arrangement with Ottenheimer Publishers, Inc.

Picture Credits

Andersen Corporation
The Bilco Company
California Redwood Association
Benjamin Moore & Company
The Black & Decker Manufacturing Company
The Asphalt Institute
United States Department of Agriculture
**Celotex, a Jim Walter Company**

# Contents

# Introduction

However well a structure is built initially, proper maintenance and repairs are necessary from time to time to keep it in first-class condition. An effective inspection will disclose whether specific types of maintenance or repairs are needed. Your maintenance program should be designed to detect deficiencies and damages promptly and to perform economical and workmanlike repairs expeditiously.

The program will be most effective if you make inspections at scheduled intervals. You should also make emergency inspections before and after unusual and severe storms that bring high-velocity winds, abnormal tides, and heavy wave action and before and after heavy snowstorms and periods of extremely low temperatures. Inspections can reveal minor defects that can be corrected promptly—before they become major defects requiring extensive repairs.

There are two general principles to keep in mind when considering repairs to the outside of your house: (1) If it is built right to begin with, your maintenance problems will be minimal, and this principle applies to every repair you make. A sloppy, inadequate repair job is guaranteed to haunt you. (2) The longer you wait to make necessary repairs, the worse the problem becomes and the more effort and money will be needed to repair the damage. Most people realize the importance of replacing a broken window promptly, and it is just as important to repair or replace defective parts of a roof or of exterior walls. Unfortunately, while it is possible to feel the wind coming through the broken window, it isn't always possible to see or feel the damage to the structure beneath a loose or broken slate. Replacing one slate is fairly easy; replacing the supporting structure of the roof is not.

Another important aspect of home repair is to know your own limitations. You can handle many repairs yourself; however, if you are not properly trained, it may be better to hire an expert. When you are attempting major repairs, it is always a good idea to consult an expert. The person who confidently begins a large repair job in the do-it-yourself spirit frequently finds that he must hire an expert to repair his repair job.

Finally, remember that your home is one of the biggest investments you will ever make. Don't allow simple neglect to ruin your investment.

# 1
# Painting Your House

Some people enjoy painting the house; for others it's a chore. But it must be done occasionally. One reason is appearance. An even more important one is protection of the wood or other exterior surfaces. Wood rots when it is not fully protected by paint or other finishes, and rotting or water-soaked wood allows moisture to reach the interior, where it can cause costly damage. Some metals rust when not protected; others develop a corrosive wash that stains surrounding surfaces. Delay, when repainting is needed, can also mean extra work when you finally do paint. Old paint that has blistered, cracked, and peeled will have to be removed before new paint can be applied.

Use materials of good quality and take time to do a good job when you paint. First, use good paint. It will give longer and better protection. The common fault of weekend painters is to buy a "bargain" paint—a bad bargain because they often find themselves repainting the house in a year or two. Second, prepare the surface properly for painting. Even the best paint won't last on a poorly prepared surface. Third, apply the paint correctly. Improper application can be as damaging as poor preparation of the surface.

## TYPES OF PAINT

There are a number of different types of exterior paint; however, selection doesn't have to be a problem.

First, consider the type of surface—wood, metal, or masonry. Some paints can be used on all three; others on two. Condition of the surface is also important. Old chalky surfaces, for example, are not generally a sound base for latex or water-based paints.

Next, consider any special requirements. For example, nonchalking paint may be advisable where chalk rundown would discolor adjacent brick or stone surfaces. Mildew may be a problem in your area; mildew-resistant paint is available. Lead-free paints can be used in areas where sulfur fumes cause staining of paints containing lead pigments.

Color is a third consideration, but it is mostly a matter of personal preference. Some colors are more durable than others, and some color combinations are more attractive than others. Your paint dealer can advise you on color durability and combinations.

# Paint Selection Chart

| | Aluminum Paint | Cement Base Paint | Exterior Clear Finish | House Paint | Metal Roof Paint | Porch-and-Deck Paint | Primer or Undercoater | Rubber Base Paint | Spar Varnish | Transparent Sealer | Trim-and-Trellis Paint | Wood Stain | Metal Primer |
|---|---|---|---|---|---|---|---|---|---|---|---|---|---|
| **WOOD** | | | | | | | | | | | | | |
| Natural finish | | | X | | | | | | X | | | X | |
| Porch floor | | | | | | X | | | | | | | |
| Shingle roof | | | | | | | | | | | | X | |
| Shutters and trim | | | | X● | | | X | | | | X● | | |
| Siding | X | | | X● | | | X | | | | | | |
| Windows | X | | | X● | | | X | | | | X● | | |
| **MASONRY** | | | | | | | | | | | | | |
| Asbestos cement | | | | X● | | | X | X | | | | | |
| Brick | X | X | | X● | | | X | X | | X | | | |
| Cement and cinder block | X | X | | X● | | | X | X | | X | | | |
| Cement porch floor | | | | | | X | | X | | | | | |
| Stucco | X | X | | X● | | | X | X | | X | | | |
| **METAL** | | | | | | | | | | | | | |
| Copper | | | | | | | | | X | | | | |
| Galvanized | X● | | | X● | | | X | | X | | X● | | X |
| Iron | X● | | | X● | | | | | | | X● | | X |
| Roofing | | | | | X● | | | | | | | | X |
| Siding | X● | | | X● | | | | | | | X● | | X |
| Windows, aluminum | X | | | X● | | | | | | | X● | | X |
| Windows, steel | X● | | | X● | | | | | | | X● | | X |

Black dot (X●) indicates that a primer or sealer may be necessary before the finishing coat or coats (unless the surface has been previously finished).

*House paint* is a commercial term used to describe exterior paints mixed with many different formulations. It is the most widely used type of paint. Formulations are available for use on all surfaces and for all special requirements such as chalk or mildew resistance. White is the most popular color. House paint contains two parts: a solid part (pigments) and a liquid part (the vehicle).

The paint is available in both oil-base and latex (water-base) types. The vehicle of oil-base paint consists usually of linseed oil with turpentine or mineral spirits as the thinner. Latex paint contains water as the vehicle thinner. Its vehicle consists of fine particles of resin emulsified or held in suspension in water.

In the past several years exterior latex paint has developed to the point where it now accounts for a significant portion of the house paint market. There are a number of reasons for this, and the primary one is the cleanability of latex both during and after painting.

| If the roof of your house is | You can paint the body | Pink | Bright red | Red-orange | Tile red | Cream | Bright yellow | Light green | Dark green | Gray-green | Blue-green | Light blue | Dark blue | Blue-gray | Violet | Br... |
|---|---|---|---|---|---|---|---|---|---|---|---|---|---|---|---|---|
| **GRAY** | White | x | x | x | x | x | x | x | x | x | x | x | x | x | x | |
| | Gray | x | x | x | x | | x | x | x | x | x | x | x | x | x | x |
| | Cream-yellow | | x | | x | | x | | x | x | | | | | | x |
| | Pale green | | | | x | | x | | x | x | | | | | | x |
| | Dark green | x | | | | x | x | x | | | | | | | | |
| | Putty | | | x | x | | | | x | x | | | x | x | x | |
| | Dull red | x | | | | x | | x | | | | | | x | | x |
| **GREEN** | White | x | x | x | x | x | x | x | x | x | x | x | x | x | x | |
| | Gray | | | x | | x | x | x | | | | | | | | x |
| | Cream-yellow | | x | | x | | | | x | x | x | | | | x | x |
| | Pale green | | | x | x | x | | x | | | | | | | | x |
| | Dark green | x | | x | | x | x | x | | | | | | | | x |
| | Beige | | | | x | | | | x | x | x | | x | x | | |
| | Brown | x | | | | x | x | x | | | | | | | | x |
| | Dull red | | | | | x | | x | | x | | | | | | x |
| **RED** | White | | x | | x | | | | x | | x | | | x | | |
| | Light gray | | x | | x | | | | x | | | | | | | x |
| | Cream-yellow | | x | | x | | | | | | x | | x | x | | |
| | Pale green | | x | | x | | | | | | | | | | | x |
| | Dull red | | | | | x | | x | | x | x | | | | | x |
| **BROWN** | White | | | x | x | | x | x | x | x | x | | x | x | x | |
| | Buff | | | | x | | | | x | x | x | | | | x | |
| | Pink-beige | | | | x | | | | x | x | | | | | x | x |
| | Cream-yellow | | | | x | | | | x | x | x | | | | x | |
| | Pale green | | | | | | | | x | x | | | | | x | |
| | Brown | | | x | | x | x | | | | | | | | | x |
| **BLUE** | White | | | x | x | | x | | | | | x | x | | | |
| | Gray | | | x | | x | | | | | | x | x | | | x |
| | Cream-yellow | | | x | x | | | | | | | | | x | x | x |
| | Blue | | | x | | x | x | | | | | x | | | | x |

*Choosing paint colors that complement each other is very important.
Don't forget to consider the color of your roof. If your house has shutters,
paint the trim either the same color as the body of the house or white.
If your house has no shutters, use these suggested colors for the trim.*

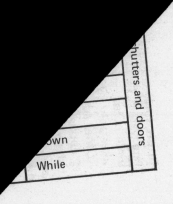

equire only
nly two to
ree surface

clude easi-
h, usually
e to alkali
pplied in

has a ve-
d oil dis-
roperties

he brand
previously if
given good service. A change is necessary only if the paint proved unsatisfactory.

## Wood Paints

The tendency of wood to expand and contract during changes in temperature and humidity makes it imperative that a good wood primer be applied to new siding to provide the necessary anchorage for the finish paint. Oil-base house paint or latex house paint is used on wood siding.

For exterior wood trim, such as windows, shutters, and doors, exterior trim paint is the favorite finish. It is an oil/alkyd/resin-base enamel. Its properties include rapid drying, high gloss, good color and gloss retention, and good durability. House paint can be used for trim, but it does not retain its gloss as long. Also, chalking may discolor adjacent surfaces.

## Masonry Paints

Exterior latex masonry paint is a standard paint for masonry. Cement-base paint may be used on unglazed brick, stucco, cement, and cinder block. Rubber-base paint and aluminum paint with the proper vehicle may also be used.

Common brick sometimes is sealed with a penetrating type of clear exterior varnish to control efflorescence and spalling (flaking or chipping of the brick). This varnish withstands weather, yet retains the natural appearance of the surface.

Old painted surfaces that have become chalky should be painted with an exterior oil primer to rebind the chalk.

*Clean and prime galvanized steel gutters and downspouts for protection.*

## Metal Paints

Zinc chromate primers are effective on copper, aluminum, and steel surfaces, but other types are also available for use on metal.

Galvanized steel surfaces, such as gutters and downspouts, should be primed with recommended special primers because conventional primers usually do not adhere well to this type of metal. A zinc-dust, zinc-oxide primer works well on galvanized steel. Exterior latex paints are sometimes used directly over galvanized surfaces, but not oil paints.

Unpainted iron and steel surfaces rust when exposed to the weather. Rust, dirt, oils and old loose paint should be removed by wire brushing or power tool cleaning. Then treat the surface with an anticorrosive primer.

Use house paint, aluminum paint, or exterior enamel on steel or aluminum windows. Paint window screens with a special screen enamel.

## Porch and Deck Paint

Porch and deck paint may be used on both concrete and wood porches and steps. On wood, a primer coat is applied first. On concrete, an alkali-resistant primer is recommended. Rubber-base paints are excellent for use on concrete floors. Hard and glossy concrete surfaces must be etched or roughened first.

## WOOD FINISHES AND STAINS

The appearance of the surface of unpainted exterior woodwork, such as the siding of a house, will change slowly if it is allowed to weather without a finish. The wood will develop the surface checks, roughening, and gray color that are characteristic of weathered wood.

You can apply finishes to the exterior woodwork of your house to maintain the original color and grain pattern (stain, sealer, or varnish), preserve the original smoothness of freshly planed lumber (varnish or paint), change the color (paint or stain), or improve the natural weathered appearance of wood (water-repellent preservative).

The first finishing job on your house is the most important one. It is the foundation for all subsequent finishing. If all goes well, it will remain there for the life of your house. Sacrificing quality of finish and finish application to reduce the initial costs very likely will lead to excessive maintenance over the years. Unfortunately, a standard grading system for finishes is not available.

There are two broad classes of finishes other than paint: natural finishes and stains. Your choice depends on personal preference, after you consider the advantages and disadvantages of each.

Natural finishes penetrate the wood or form a film or coating on its surface. These penetrating finishes may be clear or lightly pigmented. The film-forming type (varnish) usually is clear. The penetrating finishes—oil finishes, wood sealer finishes, and water-repellent preservatives—leave little or no continuous coating on the surface. Varnish gives a smooth, glossy coat.

The Forest Products Laboratory (FPL) natural finish is a recent development in penetrating natural finishes. This finish has a linseed oil vehicle and ingredients that protect the oil from mildew and the wood from excessive water entry at joints. It also has enough durable pigment to provide color but not enough to hide the grain of the wood. This type of finish is sometimes called a lightly pigmented (modified) stain.

One initial brush application of FPL natural finish normally will last about three years. Clear oil, wood sealer, or varnish finishes generally require two or three brush applications at first and need refinishing after one or two years. In addition, varnishes may need complete removal after a few refinishings to restore a satisfactory finishing surface.

Most states have regulations that require natural finishes to be resistant to mildew.

If you want to improve the natural weathered appearance of unfinished wood siding, brush or spray one application of an unpigmented water-repellent preservative solution on the siding at the start. This should be followed by reapplication of the solution at intervals of two to four years or more, depending on the appearance of the siding.

Stains penetrate and color wood. They usually are applied initially in two coats, which obscure the grain but leave little or no surface film. Rough-sawed or weathered wood surfaces are especially suitable for shingle stains and modified stains.

Good shingle stains (heavily pigmented) are inexpensive and more durable than natural finishes. Available colors are usually dark brown, green, red, and yellow.

Good stains should last at least five years on rough surfaces and may last as long as nine or ten years. Even on planed surfaces, they may last as long as paint. A second coat of stain is advisable about six to eight months after the first application, however, because there will be some checking of siding surfaces with application of the first coat. The second coat will fill the checks with stain.

Since stains form little or no coating on the surface of the wood, they do not crack, curl, flake, or blister. Some stains, however, contain creosote, which may discolor light-colored paint applied over them later.

The grade of exterior woodwork used in a house will help you determine how long a good-quality stain, finish, or paint will last. The top grade will cost more initially, but it—and the finish applied to it—will perform better, and the maintenance costs will be lower. The best grades of the more expensive woods are generally vertical grain rather than flat grain. They shrink and swell less than the lower grades and thus hold finish better. They also have fewer or no knots, pitch streaks, splits, and warp and have a more suitable moisture content for painting.

## PREPARING EXTERIOR SURFACES FOR PAINTING

Before you paint your house, you should do several things to ensure a good job. The finest paint, applied with the greatest skill, will not produce a satisfactory finish unless the surface has been properly prepared. The basic principles are simple. They vary somewhat for different surfaces and, to some extent, with different paints, but the goal is the same—to provide a surface with which the paint can make a strong, permanent bond. The following are general preparations that apply to most surfaces.

The surface must be clean, smooth, and free from dust. Use sandpaper, a wire brush, steel wool, or a scraper to remove chipped, peeled, and blistered paint. Remove oil and grease by wiping with mineral spirits. If you use a detergent, rinse the surface thoroughly with clear water.

Check the exterior of the house for chalking by running your palm over the old paint. A deposit of fine, white dust on your hand means that the paint has started to chalk, or become powdery. Badly chalked paint should be removed with a stiff bristle brush, or by scrubbing with water mixed with household washing soda or trisodium phosphate (TSP), which is sold in hardware stores. Once the house is washed, it needs to be rinsed thoroughly and

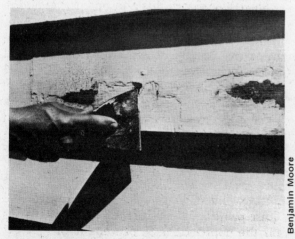

Remove chipped or blistered paint by scraping, brushing, sanding, or a combination of these techniques.

then checked for additional chalking. If chalking is still present, you should apply a coat of oil primer.

If the old surface is only moderately chalked, the primer coat should be all that is needed. The primer rebinds the loose particles and provides a solid base for the paint.

While removing the chalk, check for mildew, which will show up as dirty patches that did not come clean with the mild detergent solution. Usually a strong chlorine bleach solution with just a little detergent added will get rid of mildew. If the mildew is persistent, you might try adding trisodium phosphate and some household ammonia to the solution. Be sure to wear protective clothing when using these solutions, and then be sure to wash the solution off the house when you have finished.

Loose, cracked, or shrunken putty or caulk should be removed by scraping. If new putty, glazing compound, caulking compounds or sealants are used, they should be applied to a clean surface and allowed to harden before paint is applied. If the caulk is a latex type, latex paint can be applied over it immediately without waiting for the caulk to harden.

Damp surfaces must be allowed to dry before paint is applied, unless you are using a latex paint. Moisture on the painting surface can prevent a good bond.

### Special Preparation for Wood Surfaces

Wood siding should not contain knots or sappy streaks, but if you encounter them in new siding, clean them with turpentine and seal them with a good knot sealer. The knot sealer will seal in oily extractives and prevent staining and cracking of the paint in the knot area. Smooth any rough spots in the wood with sandpaper or another abrasive. Dust off the surface before you paint it.

Old surfaces in good condition—just slightly faded, dirty, or chalky—may only need dusting before being repainted. Very dirty surfaces should be washed with a mild synthetic detergent and rinsed thoroughly with water. Grease or other oily matter can be removed by cleaning the surface with mineral spirits.

Remove all nail rust marks by sanding. Set the nailheads below the surface, prime them, and putty the hole. Fasten loose siding with nonrusting nails. Fill all cracks, joints, and crevices with glazing compound, putty, or plastic wood. These compounds are available from paint and hardware stores. After the compound dries, sand lightly until the area is smooth and flush with the wood. Always sand in the direction of the grain, never across it.

Where cracking or blistering extends over a large area, remove all old paint down to the bare wood. Old paint can be removed by sanding, scraping, burning, or with chemical paint removers. Scraping is the simplest but hardest method. Sanding is most effective on smooth surfaces. Chemical paint remover can be expensive for large areas. Only experienced persons should attempt the burning method because it is easy to burn both the old paint and the wood under it.

Correct the condition that caused the blistering, cracking, or peeling of the old paint before you repaint. Otherwise, you may run into the same trouble again. In spots where peeling is excessive, be sure to check for leaks that have allowed moisture to get behind the siding. A good practice is to caulk all cracks around doors and windows, in the siding, and around the foundation wall. Give particular attention to joints in the guttering. If the cause of blistering, cracking, or peeling is not obvious, read the section on paint failures at the end of this chapter for diagnostic help.

New wood surfaces to be stained should first be sanded smooth in most cases. Open-grain (porous) wood should then be given a coat of paste filler. Choose a color to match the wood you are working with. The surface should be sanded again before the stain is applied.

If you plan to put stain on lumber with rough-sawn surfaces or allow it to weather naturally, do not be too concerned about small, tight knots and other minor blemishes. Minor blemishes do not greatly affect stain performance or natural weathering. Furthermore, you may like their appearance.

### Special Preparation for Metal Surfaces

New metal surfaces such as aluminum or tin should be cleaned with a solvent such as mineral spirits to remove the oil and grease applied

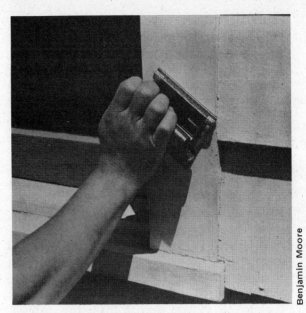

Wood surfaces that are to be stained should be sanded until they are smooth.

to the metal as a preservative by the manufacturer.

New galvanized steel surfaces should weather for about six months before being painted. If earlier painting is necessary, first wash the surface with a vinegar solution and rinse it thoroughly. This treatment will remove any manufacturing residue and stain inhibitors. Then, apply a primer recommended specifically for galvanized surfaces.

Paint will not adhere well when applied over rusted or corroded surfaces. Rust and loose paint can usually be removed from iron and steel surfaces with sandpaper, a stiff wire brush, or a power tool equipped with brushes. Chipping may be necessary in severe cases. Chemical rust removers are also available from paint and hardware stores.

Copper should be cleaned with a phosphoric acid cleaner, buffed and polished until bright, and then coated before it discolors. Copper gutters and downspouts do not, however, require painting. The protective oxide that forms on the copper surface darkens it or turns it green, but does not shorten the life of the metal. Copper is often painted to prevent staining of adjacent painted surfaces.

## Special Preparation for Masonry Surfaces

New concrete should weather for several months before being painted. If earlier painting is necessary, first wash the surface with a solvent, such as mineral spirits, to remove any grease or oil and any film left over from hardening compounds used during the curing process.

Allow new plaster to dry for thirty days before painting.

Roughen unpainted concrete and stucco with a wire brush to ensure a good bond between the surface and the paint.

Surfaces such as plaster, gypsum, cement, and drywall should be dry and clean. If the surface is cracked, sand it smooth and then fill with spackling compound or some other recommended crack filler. Pay particular attention to mortar joints. After the repaired surface is dry, sand lightly until smooth—then wipe clean.

Clean both new and old surfaces thoroughly before painting. Remove dirt and loose particles with a wire brush. Oil and grease can be removed by washing the surface with a commercial cleaner or with a detergent and water. After cleaning a surface, wash or hose it. Loose, peeling, or heavily chalked paint can be removed by sandblasting.

If the old paint is just moderately chalked but is otherwise "tight" and nonflaking, coat it with a recommended sealer or conditioner before you repaint with a water-base paint. Some latex paints are modified to allow painting over slightly chalked surfaces. Follow the manufacturer's directions.

Remove efflorescence, the crystalline deposit that appears on bricks and mortar, by using undiluted vinegar or a 5 percent muriatic acid solution. After scrubbing with acid, rinse the surface thoroughly. When using muriatic acid, wear goggles and gloves for protection.

## FIGURING YOUR PAINT ORDER

After you have a clear idea of how to go about preparing the surface, the next step is to decide how much paint to buy.

For a rough estimate, you can figure the amount of paint you need for flat surfaces by simply multiplying the height times the width and comparing the result with the coverage estimate on the label. If, for example, you want to paint a wall that has 416 square feet of area, a gallon of paint advertised as covering 500 square feet will be adequate for one coat. Second coats generally require less paint. However, these are average estimates of coverage. Some surfaces are more absorbent than others, and some methods of applying paint are more wasteful than others.

A paint dealer can help you estimate if he knows what type of surface you will be covering and the exact measurements. The dealer will also be able to advise you about the number of coats that will be required for different surfaces and different types of paint.

## GENERAL PREPARATIONS FOR PAINTING

Before you brush, roll, or spray a drop of paint, there are a few other preparations that are necessary to ensure a good job with a minimum of effort, errors, and spattering. The precautions may seem obvious, but they are often overlooked.

### Protect Other Surfaces

Cover the grass, patio, and other adjoining surfaces with drop cloths. Cover any plants that are nearby. You can use tarpaulins, old sheets, or inexpensive plastic sheets designed for the purpose. No matter how neat you are as a painter, accidents can and do happen. It is easier to protect your house and grounds than it is to try to remove half a bucket of spilled paint.

Clean up as you paint. Wet paint is easy to remove; dry paint is hard to remove. Use turpentine or another thinner to remove oil paint; use water to remove latex paint.

Rub protective cream onto your hands and arms. A film of this cream will make it easier to remove paint from your skin when the job is done. Old gloves or disposable plastic gloves and aprons are also useful.

### Check the Condition of the Paint

When you buy new paint of good quality from a reputable store, it is usually in excellent condition; however, you should examine

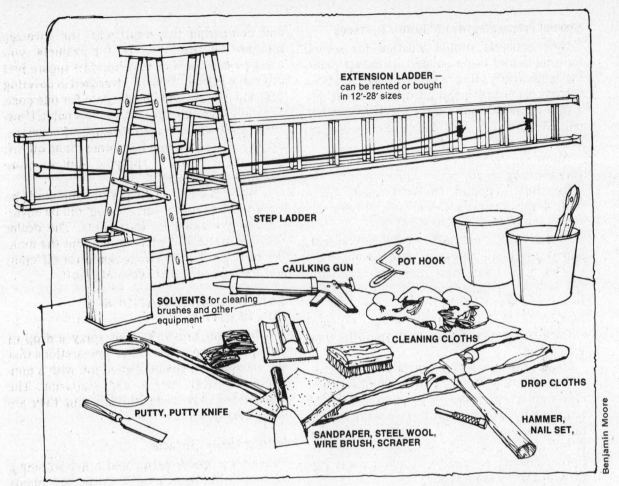

EXTENSION LADDER — can be rented or bought in 12'-28' sizes

STEP LADDER

CAULKING GUN

POT HOOK

SOLVENTS for cleaning brushes and other equipment

CLEANING CLOTHS

DROP CLOTHS

PUTTY, PUTTY KNIFE

SANDPAPER, STEEL WOOL, WIRE BRUSH, SCRAPER

HAMMER, NAIL SET,

Benjamin Moore

*Having the proper equipment at hand before you start painting helps ensure a good paint job.*

Benjamin Moore

*Put drop cloths under the area you are about to paint. Cover sidewalks as well as shrubs to save clean-up time.*

Benjamin Moore

*If paint falls on the sidewalk, clean it immediately.*

it for lumps, curdling, or color separation. Do not use if there are signs of these conditions.

Old paints—especially latex paints—that give off a foul odor when you open the container or that show signs of lumps or curdling are probably spoiled and should be discarded.

If there is a "skin" on the surface of the paint when you open the container, remove as much of the hardened film as you can with a spatula or knife and strain the paint through cheesecloth or fine wire mesh, such as window screening. If you fail to do this, bits of the skin will show up with exasperating frequency to spoil the appearance of your paint job.

### Follow Directions for Mixing

New paints are usually ready for use when purchased and require no thinning except when they are to be applied with a sprayer. Get the advice of the paint store salesman when you buy the paint, and check the label before you mix or stir. Some manufacturers do not recommend mixing because it may introduce air bubbles.

If mixing is required, it can be done at the paint store by placing the can in a mechanical agitator, or you can do it at home with a paddle or spatula.

Stir or shake oil-base paint thoroughly before you start to paint. Stir it frequently while painting. Latex or water-base paint should not be shaken because it foams.

If you open the can and find that the pigment has settled, use a clean paddle or spatula and gradually work the pigment up from the bottom of the can, using a circular stirring motion. Continue until the pigment is thoroughly and evenly distributed with no signs of color separation. If the settled layer is hard or rubbery and resists stirring, the paint is probably too old and should be discarded.

### Protect the Paint Between Jobs

Between jobs, even overnight, cover the paint container tightly to prevent evaporation and thickening and to keep dust out of the paint. Oil base and alkyd paints can develop a skin from exposure to the air.

When you finish painting, clean the rim of the paint can thoroughly and put the lid on tight. To ensure that the lid is airtight, cover the rim with a cloth or piece of plastic film (to prevent spattering) and then tap the lid firmly into place with a hammer.

### HOW TO PAINT

Start painting at a high point of the house—at a corner or under the eaves. Paint from top to bottom and then begin again at the top. Complete one sidewall before starting another. Do the walls first, then the doors, windows, and trim areas.

On windows, paint the wood dividing the glass first. Then paint the frame, trim, sill, and apron in that order. Shutters and storm sash are easier to paint if removed from the house and laid flat on supports. Wipe off dust and dirt before painting them.

Follow the sun around the house, if possible, so that you will be painting in the shade. This technique will result in a more satisfactory paint job because the paint will not dry out too rapidly.

To avoid future separation between coats of paint, called intercoat peeling, apply the first top coat within two weeks after the primer and the second top coat within two weeks of the first.

To avoid temperature blistering, do not apply oil-base paints on a cool surface that will be heated by the sun within a few hours.

Repaint only when the old paint has worn thin and no longer protects the surface below. The color of faded or dirty paint can often be restored by washing. Where wood surfaces are exposed, spot prime with a zinc-free linseed oil primer before repainting.

Too-frequent repainting builds up an excessively thick coating that is more sensitive to the deteriorating effects of the weather. Ordinarily, every four years will be often enough to repaint a house.

Sheltered areas, such as eaves and porch ceilings, may not need repainting every time the body of the house is repainted; every other time may be sufficient.

To do a good job with a minimum of trouble, choose the right tools and learn how to handle them properly. The brush, the roller, and the sprayer are the basic work tools.

*Choose brushes and rollers that do the job most efficiently and save you the most time.*

*Hold the brush at an angle and apply moderate pressure to spread paint evenly and smoothly.*

## Using a Brush

The use of a brush assures good contact of paint with pores, cracks and crevices. Brushing is particularly recommended for applying primer coats and exterior paints.

In selecting a brush you should choose one that is wide enough to cover the area in a reasonable amount of time. If you are painting large areas such as exterior walls, you will want a wide brush—probably 4 to 5 inches in width. If you are painting windows or trim, you will want a narrower brush (probably 1 inch to 1½ inches wide) so that you can handle comparatively narrow surfaces.

The bristles should be reasonably long and thick so that they will hold a good load of paint. They should be flexible so that you can stroke evenly and smoothly. Generally speaking, a medium-priced brush is the best investment if you paint only occasionally.

If you are using a gallon of paint, transfer it to a larger container or pour about half into another container. It will be easier to handle and there will be room for the brush. Dip your brush to about a third of the length of the bristles. Tap off excess paint on the inside of the can; do not scrape the brush across the rim.

Paint should be brushed up and down, then across for even distribution. On a rough surface, especially, it is wise to vary the direction of the strokes so that the paint will penetrate thoroughly. On wood siding, however, the finishing strokes should follow the wood grain.

The brush should be held at a slight angle when applying the paint, and pressure should be moderate and even. Excessive pressure or "stuffing" the brush into corners and cracks may damage the bristles. Ues long, sweeping arm strokes, keeping an even pressure on the brush. Apply both sides of each brushful. End each stroke with a light, lifting motion.

Always work toward the "wet edge" of the previously painted area, making sure not to try to cover too much surface with each brushload. When you finish an area, go over it with light, quick strokes to smooth brush marks and to recoat any thin spots.

A good brush is an expensive tool, and it pays to invest the necessary time and effort to take care of it properly. Clean brushes immediately after use with a thinner or special brush cleaner recommended by your paint or hardware dealer. Use turpentine or mineral spirits to remove oil-base paints, enamels, and varnish. Remove latex paints promptly from brushes with soap and water. If paint is allowed to dry on a brush, a paint remover or brush-cleaning solvent will be needed.

## Using a Roller

For large, flat surfaces, painting by roller is easier than painting by brush for the average do-it-yourself painter. Select a roller with a comfortable-to-hold handle and try several dry sweeps across the surface until you get the hang of it.

When you buy a roller, you find that it comes as part of a set—the roller itself, and a sloping metal or plastic tray. Pour paint into the tray until approximately two-thirds of the corrugated bottom is covered.

Dip the roller into the paint in the shallow section of the tray, and roll it back and forth until it is well covered. If the roller drips when you lift it from the tray, it is overloaded.

*Remove excess paint with a scraper, soak the brush in the proper thinner and work it against the bottom of a container.*

*To loosen paint in the center of the brush, squeeze the bristles between your thumb and forefinger, then rinse again in thinner. If necessary, work the brush in mild soapsuds, then rinse in clear water.*

*Press out the water in the brush with a stick.*

*Twirl the brush in a container so that you won't get splashed.*

*Comb bristles carefully, including those below the surface. Suspend the brush from the handle or lay it flat on a clean surface to dry. Wrap the dry brush in the original wrapper or in heavy paper to keep the bristles straight. Suspend it by the handle or lay it flat to store it.*

Squeeze out some of the paint by pressing the roller against the upper part of the tray above the paint line.

Apply paint by moving the roller back and forth over the surface being painted—first up and down in long, even strokes, then across. Reload the roller with paint as needed.

Rollers used with alkyd or oil-base paints should be cleaned with turpentine or mineral spirits. When latex paint has been used, soap and water will do a satisfactory cleaning job. If any kind of paint has been allowed to dry on the roller, a paint remover or brush-cleaning solvent will be needed.

## Using a Paint Sprayer

Paint sprayers are particularly useful for large areas. Spraying is much faster than brushing or rolling. Although some paint will probably be wasted through overspraying, the time and effort saved may more than compensate for any additional paint cost. Once you have perfected your spraying technique, you can produce a coating with excellent uniformity in thickness and appearance.

Surface areas that are difficult to reach with a brush or roller can easily be covered by the sprayer. All coats can be applied satisfactorily by the spray technique except for the primer coats. Spraying should be done only on a clean surface because the paint may not adhere well if a dust film is present.

Preparation of the paint is of critical importance when a sprayer is to be used. Stir or strain the paint to remove any lumps, and thin it carefully. If the paint is lumpy or too thick, it may clog the spray valve; if it is too thin, the paint may sag or run after it is applied. Follow the manufacturer's instructions on the paint label for the type and amount of thinner to be used.

Before you begin, ask your paint dealer to show you exactly how the sprayer works, and to give you pointers on how to use it to best advantage.

For best results, adjust the width of the spray fan to the size of the surface to be coated. A narrow fan is best for spraying small or narrow surfaces; a wider fan should be used to spray walls.

While using proper techniques to spray paint, this man neglected to use drop cloths to cover the area.

Before spraying, test the thickness of the paint, the size of the fan, and the motion of the spray gun on a waste board before painting any other surface. Spraying paint too thickly can cause rippling of the wet film or lead to blistering later.

Hold the nozzle about eight inches from the surface to be painted. Start the stroke or motion of the hand holding the sprayer while the spray is pointed slightly beyond the surface to be painted. This assures a smooth, even flow when you reach the surface to be coated.

Move the sprayer parallel to the surface, moving with an even stroke back and forth across the area. Spray corners and edges first. Use a respirator to avoid inhaling the vapors.

Be sure to cover everything close to the work area with drop cloths, tarps, or newspapers. The "bounceback" from a sprayer may extend several feet from the work surface.

The sprayer should be cleaned promptly—before the paint dries in it. After using oil-base or alkyd paints, clean the sprayer with the same solvent used to thin the paint. After using latex paint, clean the sprayer with detergent and water. Fill the sprayer tank with the cleaning liquid and spray it clean.

If the sprayer tip becomes clogged, clean it with a broom straw. Never use a wire or a nail to clear clogged air holes in the sprayer tip.

## NUMBER OF COATS

Three coats of paint are recommended for new wood surfaces—one primer and two finish coats. Two-coat application is sometimes used and gives long service when the paints are correctly chosen and properly applied.

On old surfaces in good condition, one top coat may be sufficient. But if the paint is very thin, apply two top coats.

On bare surfaces, surfaces with very little paint left on them, or very chalky surfaces, apply a primer and two top coats.

Use a good-quality oil-base exterior primer with solvent-thinned paint. Most manufacturers recommend use of a solvent-thinned primer with latex or water-base paint. A solvent-thinned primer may be applied to a dry surface only. Prime after you clean and repair the surface but before you putty cracks.

Allow the primer coat to dry according to the manufacturer's label instructions. Allow longer drying time in humid weather. Apply the finish coats as soon as the primer has dried sufficiently. (If you must wait a month or more, wash the surface thoroughly before applying the top coats.) Allow about forty-eight hours' drying time between oil-base finish coats. Two coats of latex paint may be applied in one day.

On metal surfaces, prime both new metal and old metal from which the paint has been removed. Good primers usually contain zinc dust, red lead, zinc yellow, blue lead, iron oxide, or some rust-inhibiting pigment. After the primer has dried sufficiently, apply one or two finish coats of paint.

## WHEN TO PAINT

You can easily ruin your paint job if you forget to consider the weather. Excessive humidity or extremely cold weather can cause you trouble. If humidity is high, check the surface before painting. If you feel a film of moisture on the surface, wait for a better day.

Exterior painting is not recommended if the temperature is below 50° or above 95°F. because you may not be able to get a good bond. This is especially critical if using latex paint.

Latex and water-base paints allow more freedom in application than oil-base paints. They can be applied in humid weather and to damp surfaces. But for best results with either type of paint, do your painting when the weather is clear and dry and the temperature is between 50° and 90°F.

Don't paint in windy or dusty weather or at times when insects may get caught in the paint. Insects are usually the biggest problem during fall evenings. Don't try to remove insects from wet paint; brush them off after the paint dries.

Start painting after the morning dew or frost has evaporated. Stop painting in late afternoon or early evening on cool fall days. This is more important with oil-base paint than with latex paint. In hot weather, paint a surface after it has been exposed to the sun and is in the shade.

Ideally, the north side of the building should be painted in the first part of the morning, the east side later in the morning, the south side in the first part of the afternoon, and the west side later in the afternoon.

## SAFETY PRECAUTIONS

Working on a ladder or on scaffolding is always dangerous. Observe these precautions:

1. Make sure that the ladder is not defective. Check the rungs and side rails carefully. Check ropes and pulleys to be sure they are securely fastened and work properly.
2. Be sure that the ladder is positioned firmly—both on the ground and against the house. Set the foot of the ladder away from the wall one-fourth of the distance to the point of support. If you use scaffolding, make sure that it is secure.
3. Always face the ladder when climbing up or down. Hold on with both hands. Carry tools in your pocket or haul them up with a line.
4. Be sure that the paint bucket, tools, and other objects are secure when you are on a ladder or scaffolding. Falling objects can injure persons walking below.
5. Do not overreach when painting. Move the ladder frequently rather than risking a fall.

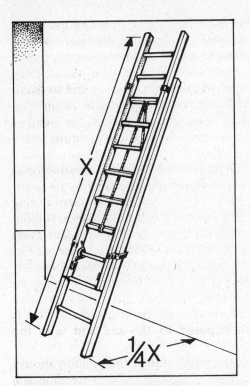
*Set the ladder at a safe angle when you paint.*

Benjamin Moore

*Keep your body between the rails when painting.*

A good rule is to keep your belt buckle between the side rails.

6. Lean toward the ladder when working. Keep one hand free—ready to grab the ladder just in case.

7. Watch for and avoid any electrical wiring within the work area. This precaution is especially important if using a metal ladder.

## PAINT FAILURES

There are a number of common paint failures. Some can be avoided simply by following the directions on the label of the paint can. Others can be avoided only by proper maintenance and sometimes by repairs.

### Blistering and Peeling

To avoid wrinkling and loss of gloss with oil-base paint, do not paint in the evenings of cool spring and fall days. That is when heavy dews frequently form before the surface of the paint has dried.

Temperature blistering, which occurs when a cool surface is painted shortly before it is heated by the sun, is most common with dark paints. The blisters are usually in the top coat of paint, and they occur within one or two days after painting. Temperature blisters do not contain water.

Blistering and peeling can also be caused by water. In fact, the two most common water-related problems are extractive staining and blistering and peeling of paint.

When too much water gets into paint or wood, moisture blisters normally appear first. Cracking and peeling follow. Sometimes the paint peels without blistering. Sometimes the blisters go unnoticed.

Moisture blisters usually contain water when they form or soon afterward. Eventually they dry out. Small blisters may disappear on drying. Fairly large ones may leave a rough spot on the surface. The paint may peel if the blistering is severe.

Young, thin coatings are more apt to blister before peeling because of too much moisture

USDA Photo

*Before you repaint, determine the cause of blistering and correct it.*

than are old, thick coatings, which often crack and peel without blistering.

Construction features that reduce water damage to outside paint are a wide roof overhang; wide flashing under shingles at roof edges; effective vapor barriers in ceilings and sidewalls, on top of the ground in crawl spaces, under floor slabs, and outside the foundation walls below grade; adequate and properly hung eaves troughs and downspouts; and adequate ventilation of the inside of the house, including the attic space. If these features are lacking, blistering and peeling may occur.

The first step in solving a water-related problem is to determine the source of the water that does the damage. The possible sources are outside water working in; inside water working out; and inside water vapor passing through the walls, condensing, and soaking into the exterior wood (cold-weather condensation).

Clues to moisture blistering and peeling caused by rain or dew going through joints and end grain are the following:

1. It occurs after rain or heavy dew.
2. Rain damage is worst on the sides of the building that face the prevailing winds.
3. It occurs only on woodwork that can be wetted by rain or dew.
4. It can occur on unheated or heated buildings.
5. It will be concentrated around end grain and joints.

Rain leaking through the roof obviously causes damage, but rain damage often appears to be caused by condensation or inside water leaks. Water stains on the inner side of the roof boards are the best indication of roof leaks. Often the stains indicate where the water goes after getting in.

Ice dams at horizontal roof edges and in roof valleys block the flow of melting snow and permit the water to work in under the shingles and through the roof boards. Damage resulting from them will usually occur on the wall beneath their location. The inner surface of roof boards over the eaves and under the valleys will show water stains if water is getting in because of ice dams.

Blistering or peeling of exterior paint also can be caused by plumbing leaks, overflow of sinks or bathtubs, leaky shower walls, and so forth.

Blistering and peeling caused by cold-weather condensation can be recognized by the following clues:

1. It is usually most severe on the coldest (north) side of the building or on the outside walls of unheated rooms.
2. It is likely to be concentrated on the outside walls of rooms having high humidity, such as bathrooms, kitchens, or bedrooms in which vaporizers are used.
3. The blisters appear in late winter or early spring.
4. The damage occurs on wood sheltered from wetting by outside water as well as on unprotected wood.
5. The damage occurs only on heated buildings.

These clues are not foolproof. Blistering and peeling caused by outside water, cold-weather condensation, or inside water may occur in the same place.

If the damage is caused by outside water that gets in, take the following steps:

1. Apply water-repellent preservative to all joints before repainting.
2. Caulk or putty open joints and cracks.
3. Check eaves troughs for cleanliness, slope, and capacity.
4. Repair roof leaks.
5. Check downspouts to see if they are plugged.
6. Ice should not be allowed to form at roof edges and valleys. Removing the snow will prevent this.

Joints that show damage from rain or dew need treating with water-repellent preservative before repainting. Apply water-repellent preservative as follows:

1. Remove loose paint from wood.
2. Brush the water-repellent preservative into the joints and end grain. Brushing it on the

*Caulking joints and cracks helps weatherproof the house and prevent moisture seepage.*

paint will do no good and will waste solution.

3. Wipe off excess solution with a rag.
4. Allow two days of good drying weather before repainting.

If the moisture blistering and peeling is caused by cold-weather condensation, these steps should be taken:

1. Reduce vapor penetration by painting the interior surfaces of the outside walls and ceilings. Aluminum paint works well and can be painted over with decorative paints.
2. Lower the humidity in the house as follows: Shut off humidifiers. Vent clothes dryers and kitchen and bathroom exhaust fans to the outside. Use a dehumidifier if necessary. Ventilation in the attic and a ground cover in the crawl space will cut down on the moisture inside the building.
3. Apply a zinc-free oil primer where paint has peeled to the wood surface, and then one topcoat of paint overall.

Water-soluble cover extractives occur naturally in western red cedar and redwood. The heartwood of these two species owes its attractive color, good stability, and natural decay resistance to extractives.

Discoloration occurs when the extractives are dissolved and leached from the wood by water. When the solution of extractives reaches the painted surface, the water evaporates, leaving a reddish-brown stain.

The water that gets behind the paint to cause moisture blisters also causes movement of extractives. Use the time of occurrence and distribution of the stains in the way indicated for moisture blisters to determine the source of the water. Follow the same procedures to eliminate it.

Emulsion paints and so-called breather oil paints are more porous than conventional oil paints. If these paints are used on new wood without a good oil primer, or if any paint is applied too thin on new wood, rain or even heavy dew can reach the wood easily by direct penetration of the paint coating. The extractives will come to the surface of the paint when the wood dries.

It is difficult to get a thick coating of paint on the high points of rough surfaces, such as machine-grooved shakes and rough-sawn lumber siding. Extractive staining is more likely to occur on such surfaces due to penetration of water through the coating. The reddish brown extractive will be less conspicuous if dark paints are used.

### Cross-Grain Cracking

Repainting too frequently produces an excessively thick film that is more sensitive to weather damage. Thickly built-up paint is also likely to crack abnormally across the grain. The grain of the paint is the direction of the last brush strokes. Complete paint removal is the only cure for cross-grain cracking. Then properly prime and repaint the bare wood.

### Mildew

Mildew may occur where continuously warm and damp weather prevails. Emulsion paints are more susceptible to mildew than oil paints unless they contain an effective mildewcide. Molds feed on the oil and minerals in the paint and cause a dirty-looking discoloration. They may penetrate the paint film deeply, even to the underlying wood.

To remove mildew, wash the surface one or more times with a solution of $2/3$ cup of trisodium phosphate, $1/3$ cup of detergent, and

1 quart of household bleach; add enough water to make 1 gallon. Wear rubber gloves when using this solution.

Mildew-resistant paints in all colors are available at paint and hardware stores. Manufacturers formulate these paints with fungicides or other compounds to combat mildew attack. Wear rubber gloves when using these paints.

Adding zinc oxide or spar varnish to oil paint makes it less susceptible to mildew, because it makes the paint dry to a hard film. These materials tend to make the paint brittle, however. On aging, the paint may then peel.

## Intercoat Peeling

Intercoat peeling usually is caused by lack of adhesion between the top coat and undercoats. Perhaps the primer and top coat were incompatible, the surface was too smooth or glossy, or oil or grease were not removed.

To avoid intercoat peeling, allow no more than two weeks between coats in two-coat repainting. Do not repaint more often than every four years. Do not repaint sheltered areas, such as eaves and porch ceilings, every time the weathered body of the house is painted. Repainting the sheltered areas every other time is recommended. Use primers and top coats of the same brands. It is helpful to wash the sheltered areas with a trisodium phosphate solution before repainting.

Intercoat peeling usually gets worse with time, and complete paint removal is often the only cure. After the paint has been removed, sand and prime bare surfaces, then paint.

## Excessive Chalking

Some paints are supposed to chalk, but heavy chalking may occur when poor quality paint was used, when the paint was improperly applied, or when the paint was thinned excessively. Chalking may also occur when paint is applied in rain, fog, or mist.

Chalk can be removed with a stiff, bristle brush. It can also be removed by washing the surface with mineral spirits. Apply two coats of good-quality paint. Allow three days drying time between coats.

## MAINTENANCE OF FINISHES
### Repainting or Restaining

Hot summer sun, wind-driven rain, hail, dust, and snow and ice gradually take a toll on even the best finish. How frequently the finish should be renewed is governed by the rate at which it weathers away.

As pointed out, a paint maintenance program is determined by the kind of paint used in the first paint job. The basic rule is paint only after most of the old paint film has weathered away. Always remember that coating thickness can build up dangerously if paint, especially oil-base paint, is applied too frequently. Abnormal behavior spells trouble and possibly costly removal of old paint by blowtorch or by paint and varnish remover.

Paint that starts to crack and peel from the wood indicates that a serious moisture problem may be involved. It may indicate two conditions: (1) either a primer was used that was sensitive to water and perhaps too porous to provide adequate protection from rain and dew or (2) moisture from cold-weather condensation or ice dams is excessively wetting the walls and the siding.

Quality latex paints properly applied to old painted surfaces are proving to be excellent refinish systems. Latex does not always bond well to chalked surfaces, and because of its porosity it holds rain and dew. In turn, this moisture can penetrate the paint film and produce an abnormal peeling problem. When repainting chalky surfaces with exterior latex, therefore, it is advisable either to remove the chalk by sanding, scrubbing, or steel wooling or to apply a new coat of oil-base primer over the chalk. Recent developments in latex paint formulation have greatly improved performance over old paint. Thus, it is important to read the directions on a label carefully before applying latex over old chalky paint.

Penetrating natural stains are easy to renew. Fresh finish is simply applied when the old finish appears to need it. As with the first finishing job, any excess of stain or oil should be wiped off, so that formation of a surface coat is prevented.

# 2
# Septic Tanks

A septic tank system, properly installed and maintained, generally is a satisfactory way to dispose of sewage from a household when connection to a public sewerage system is not possible, adequate land is available for absorption of the effluent, and the system is adequately separated from adjoining properties or sources of water supply. It should handle all the sewage from a normal household.

Individual septic tank and soil absorption systems are most frequently used in rural areas and in some unsewered suburban residential areas. A septic tank system will serve a home satisfactorily only if it is properly designed and installed and adequately maintained. Even a good system that doesn't have proper care and attention can become a nuisance, a burdensome expense, and a health hazard.

When septic tank systems are improperly designed or maintained, the liquid wastes may overflow to the ground surface or the plumbing in the house may be stopped up or otherwise affected. These overflows not only create offensive odors, but they are also a very serious health hazard. Sewage can contain dysentery, infectious hepatitis, typhoid, and other infectious disease organisms. Ponded sewage creates breeding places for mosquitoes and other insects.

The purpose of a septic tank is primarily to condition household wastes so that they can be more readily percolated into the subsoil. Household sewage consists of water-carried wastes from the bathroom, kitchen, laundry, floor drains, and other plumbing fixtures. It includes human excreta, toilet paper, dishwater, food scraps, wash water, bits of soap, grease, hair, cloth fibers, bleach, cleaning compounds, sweepings, and the like. It may also include ground food wastes and backwash from regenerating water-conditioning equipment.

Paper cartons, wrappers, newspapers, sticks and stones, and discarded clothing are rubbish, not sewage, and should be kept out of sewage disposal systems. Storm drainage from roofs and areaways also should be kept out of septic tank systems and other sewage disposal facilities.

A complete system consists of the house sewer, the septic tank, the effluent sewer, and the disposal or absorption area.

SCUM
LIQUID
SOLIDS

*Solids in the tank sink to the bottom; liquids and scum rise to the top.*

*Septic tank system in relation to a house*

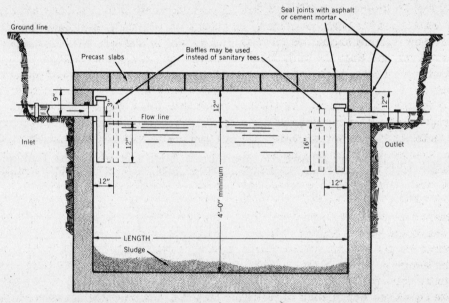

Ground line

Seal joints with asphalt or cement mortar

Precast slabs

Baffles may be used instead of sanitary tees

9″
3″
Flow line
12″
12″
16″
12″

Inlet

4′-0″ minimum

12″

Outlet

LENGTH
Sludge

*A cross section of a concrete septic tank*

A septic tank is a watertight compartment in which organic solids are decomposed by natural bacterial processes. The flow of sewage through the tank is slow, so that heavier solids settle to the bottom and accumulate as sludge. Grease and lighter particles rise to the surface and form a partly submerged scum.

The partially treated sewage, or effluent, flowing from the tank still contains large amounts of harmful bacteria and organic matter in a finely divided state or in solution. Final disposal of the effluent in the subsurface soil absorption system is also necessary.

The outlet of the tank is designed to prevent passage of floating scum and settled sludge. Liquid leaving the tank flows from a depth which traps the scum and sludge in the tank. This is usually accomplished by a baffle or submerged pipe outlet.

As a charge of sewage enters the tank from the house sewer, it displaces an equal volume of conditioned effluent, which is discharged through the effluent sewer to the absorption area.

Within the tank, the trapped materials undergo putrefaction and decomposition due to the action of bacteria that are found naturally in the sewage. Therefore, it is not necessary to add any compounds or ingredients for this purpose.

## INSPECTING AND CLEANING

The septic tank is a simple holding compartment with a capacity of about 750 to 1,000 gallons. This includes capacity for garbage disposal units and automatic washers. Some codes do not provide for the use of these appliances, and the tank size required would be 50 percent smaller.

Regardless of its capacity, the tank eventually has to be cleaned to prevent the bypass of sludge or scum which would clog the soil absorption area of the system. How often? Two- to five-year intervals should be sufficient, but this can only be learned through your family's experience. A new system should be cleaned after about one year, and then the tank should be inspected at least once a year and cleaned when necessary.

Although it is difficult for most homeowners, actual inspection of sludge and scum accumulations is the only way to determine definitely when a tank needs to be cleaned or pumped. When a tank is inspected, the depth of the sludge and scum should be measured in the vicinity of the outlet baffle. The tank should be cleaned in either of these cases: the bottom of the scum mat is within approximately 3 inches of the bottom of the outlet device, or the sludge is within 8 or 10 inches of the bottom of the outlet pipe.

Scum can be measured with a stick to which a weighted flap has been hinged, or with any device that can be used to feel out the bottom of the scum mat. The stick is forced through the mat, the hinged flap falls into a horizontal position, and the stick is raised until resistance from the bottom of the scum can be felt. With the same tool, you can find the distance to the bottom of the outlet device.

A long stick wrapped with rough, white toweling and lowered to the bottom of the tank will show the depth of sludge and the depth of the liquid in the tank. The stick should be lowered behind the outlet device to avoid scum particles. After several minutes, if you remove the stick carefully you will be able to tell how deep the sludge is because of sludge particles clinging to the toweling.

In most communities where septic tanks are used, there are firms that specialize in cleaning them. It is best to negotiate the price before the job is started. Unscrupulous operators have been known to charge by volume and then recirculate liquid or add water to "clean" the tank. The tank does not need to be flushed or hosed down, but rather emptied.

To facilitate cleaning and maintenance, the homeowner should have a diagram of his septic tank system, showing the location of the house, the septic tank manholes, the piping, and the soil absorption system.

Cleaning is usually accomplished by pumping the contents of the tank into a tank truck. Tanks should not be washed or disinfected after pumping. A small residue of sludge should be left in the tank for seeding purposes. The material that is removed can be buried in uninhabited areas or, with the permission of the proper authority, emptied into

| Liquid capacity of tank, gallons a | Liquid depth | | | |
|---|---|---|---|---|
| | 2½ feet | 3 feet | 4 feet | 5 feet |
| | Distance from bottom of outlet device to top of sludge, inches | | | |
| 750 | 5 | 6 | 10 | 13 |
| 900 | 4 | 4 | 7 | 10 |
| 1,000 | 4 | 4 | 6 | 8 |

a Tanks smaller than the capacities listed will require more frequent cleaning.

*The frequency with which the septic tank should be cleaned depends on the sludge accumulation. If your tank is smaller than the ones mentioned in the chart, it will require more frequent cleaning.*

## Devices for Measuring Sludge and Scum

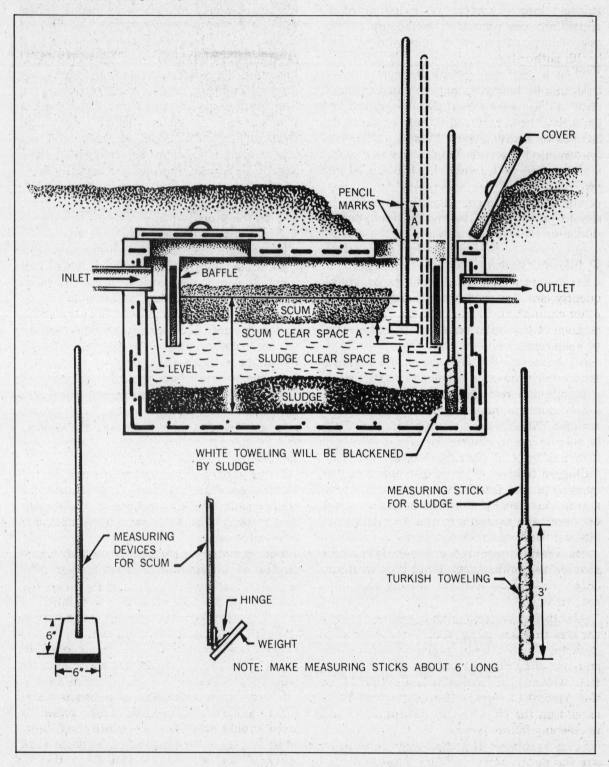

COVER

PENCIL MARKS

INLET

BAFFLE

SCUM

SCUM CLEAR SPACE A

SLUDGE CLEAR SPACE B

LEVEL

OUTLET

SLUDGE

WHITE TOWELING WILL BE BLACKENED BY SLUDGE

MEASURING STICK FOR SLUDGE

MEASURING DEVICES FOR SCUM

TURKISH TOWELING

HINGE

WEIGHT

3'

6"

6"

NOTE: MAKE MEASURING STICKS ABOUT 6' LONG

a sanitary sewer system. It should never be emptied into storm drains or discharged directly into any stream or watercourse. Methods of disposal should be approved by local health authorities.

When a large septic tank is being cleaned, care should be taken not to enter the tank until it has been thoroughly ventilated and gases have been removed to prevent explosion hazards or asphyxiation of the workers. Anyone entering the tank should have one end of a stout rope tied around his waist, with the other end held above ground by another person strong enough to pull him out if he should be overcome by any gas remaining in the tank.

## COMMON PROBLEMS

Septic tanks and soil absorption systems frequently are damaged when heavy trucks or other equipment drive over them. An accurate diagram of the system enables the homeowner to keep heavy vehicles away from the critical area. A line of cast iron pipe instead of tile should be installed under any necessary crossings for heavy vehicles.

The most common trouble with septic tank systems is the clogging of the absorption field. It may be due to improper design or construction, improper use, or neglect of servicing.

Clogged fields can sometimes be cleared by opening up and flushing the disposal lines with a hose, but usually it will be necessary to dig up, clean, and lay them in new locations.

Sewer lines also clog, usually because of roots. Cleaning with a root cutter will remove roots in the sewer but will not prevent future entry. Prevention requires making the joints root-tight.

Absorption systems of all types begin to fail the day they are put in use. A mat or crust of decaying organic slimes, precipitated minerals, and bacteria coats the bottom of the absorption system. This makes it less permeable to the passage of liquid. The coating begins to extend up the sides of the absorption system as creeping failure begins.

Some systems fail prematurely because the site was poorly selected. Many subsoils are not sufficiently permeable to transmit and absorb

*Sewage effluent rising above the soil causes a disagreeable odor and sanitary hazards.*

USDA—Soil Conservation Service

large volumes of effluent. At other locations, a seasonally high water table may occur and defeat the absorption system—forcing effluent to the surface during every wet season.

Some soil absorption systems fail prematurely because of poor construction. Heavy equipment can compact the soil, reducing its porosity and permeability. Mechanical diggers or shovels can smear the trench or pit wall and bottom with clay particles—effectively reducing its ability to transmit water.

In a properly constructed disposal system, surface water should be diverted so that rainfall will not flood out the system.

If the subsoil is sufficiently porous and if the clogging mat formation does not become too dense and thick to pass liquid, the absorption system may have a useful life expectancy of several years.

Mat formation can be controlled by maintaining an intermittent flow of sewage. The mat or crust becomes most dense and clogs the soil when it is continually wet. Much of the original absorption capacity will return if it is possible to let the mat dry out.

The system should not be left uncovered in a rain. Small particles of silt and clay may wash in and clog it.

When a trench or absorption bed is backfilled, a barrier of decomposable paper or straw should cover the stone until the fill material has a chance to stabilize. Without such a barrier, the silt and clay particles in the fill will wash down into the stone and clog it.

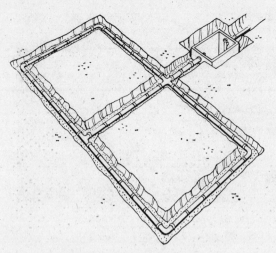

*For an absorption system in level ground, use a closed or continuous tile arrangement.*

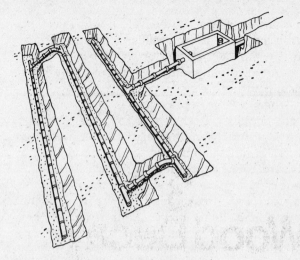

*Use a serial distribution arrangement for an absorption system in sloping ground.*

It may surprise you, but the volume of effluent discharged to the absorption system exceeds by several times the rainfall the same area may receive. In addition, the sewage discharge is more or less constant when compared to rainfall, which occurs intermittently allowing the soil to dry out between rainy periods.

It is not really surprising that absorption systems fail. Reducing the volume of water is the easiest way to prolong a system's life.

Check the footing drain sump and the sump for the laundry tray if you have one. Is ground water entering the plumbing system and being pumped to the sewerage system for disposal? No rainwater should get to the system.

When failure does occur, you have a chance to evaluate the system and your use of it. First, make sure that the absorption system really has failed. Stoppage can occur between the house and the system due to an obstruction in the sewer. Diapers, toys, children's shoes, and tree roots are common offenders—along with broken or collapsed sewer pipe. If the absorption system is at fault, effluent usually appears on the surface near the system's low end.

When the system was built, it may have been the lowest-priced arrangement acceptable to the local authorities and the building industry. Let us say you have not been wasting water to the system needlessly. If you had four or five years of trouble-free service before the first failure, that's not too bad. The prorated cost isn't exorbitant, and you have every assurance you can rebuild the system at less than its first cost. Replacing or rebuilding the absorption part of the system should make it as good as new.

Keep the original absorption system dry, and in a matter of months it should return to serviceability. Switching from one system to the other after long rest periods will prolong the life of both systems.

If you have had the septic tank cleaned routinely, cleaning at the time of failure is not necessary. The failure is in the absorption system. Cleaning the tank will give only a few days of relief.

If you are wasting water, cut down drastically. Send the laundry out or take it to a laundromat until your new absorption system is installed. Don't waste money on septic tank additives. These additives are not known to add to the life of the system, and the bacteria needed by the system are naturally found in the sewage.

Failure after the first year or two of use is bad news unless you have been wasting a lot of water to the system. If the absorption system fails despite precautions and no construction defect is apparent, you need some expert advice.

# 3
# Wood Decay

Seasoned wood, properly used, is a dependable building material. In houses that are well built and well maintained, decay causes little damage. Most damage can be avoided. Prevention is cheap; cure is sometimes costly.

## CAUSE OF DAMAGE

Wood decay is caused by minute plants called fungi. These plants consist of microscopic threads that are visible to the naked eye only when many of them occur together, but it is easy to see the fruiting bodies of fungi, from which their spores are distributed. Some fungi merely discolor wood, but decay fungi destroy the fiber. Decayed wood is often dry in the final stages but not during the process of decay. Fungi cannot work in dry wood. For this reason, there is no such thing as "dry rot," and decay is a minor problem in the driest parts of the country.

Two species of fungi spread from moist soil or wood into dry wood by conducting water to the dry wood through vinelike structures. Occasionally they cause great damage to buildings, but fortunately most fungi cannot conduct moisture in this way.

Fungi and termites may sometimes work in the same wood. Decay fungi soften the wood and, in the final stages, make it spongy or cause it to shrink or to crack and crumble. No fungi produce the continuous, clearcut tunnels or galleries characteristic of termite infestation, however.

Serious decay damage is most often due to one or more of the following errors in construction or maintenance:

1. Undrained soil and insufficient ventilation under houses without basements.
2. Wood such as grade stakes, concrete forms, or stumps left on or in the soil under houses.
3. Wood parts of the house in direct contact with the soil, especially at dirt-filled porches.
4. Wood parts embedded in masonry near the ground.
5. Use of unseasoned and infected lumber.
6. Sheathing paper that is not sufficiently impermeable to moisture vapor.

*A gill fungus*

7. Inadequate flashing at windows, doors, and roof edges.
8. Poor joinery around windows and doors and at corners, and inadequate paint maintenance.
9. Lack of rain gutters, and a roof without overhang.
10. Unventilated attics.
11. Roof leaks; leaks around shower-bathtub combinations and kitchen fixtures, and in laundry rooms.
12. Failure to use preservative-treated or naturally durable wood where moisture cannot be controlled.

## GENERAL SAFEGUARDS

To prevent decay, keep decay fungi from entering the lower part of the structure. Use dry wood as much as is practical, and build in a way that will keep wood dry most of the time. Spores or "seeds" of decay fungi are always present in the air; they cannot be kept away from wood. However, fungi can grow in wood only when it contains more than 20 percent moisture. Air-dry wood is regularly below this danger point.

### Use of Dry Lumber

Use only seasoned and sound lumber. Compared with green lumber, it has better nail-holding capacity, shrinks and warps less, and is safer from decay. Store lumber off the ground and protect it from rain.

If only green material can be obtained, it should be open-piled and allowed to dry as thoroughly as possible before it is used. The piles should be supported off the ground, and the layers should be separated from each other by narrow strips of 1-inch dry lumber. Space the boards in each layer to let air move around them on all sides. If the piles cannot be put under cover, slope them toward one end. Overlap the boards in the top layer and extend them out at the front and back to keep rain off the boards beneath. Green lumber requires sixty days or more for thorough seasoning, but even a shorter period of seasoning will decrease the chance of decay.

Particularly avoid infected lumber that is wet. It is especially dangerous where the lumber is enclosed so that it cannot dry. Wood infected heavily by stain fungi should also be avoided because it often contains decay fungi as well.

### Protection Against Rain

Roofs with considerable overhang, both at eaves and gable ends, give more protection to the rest of the house than those with narrow overhang. In fact, a good roof overhang can do much to offset decay hazards in siding and around windows and doors. As a rule, an overhang of 12 inches is desirable for a one-story house. In regions with heavy snow, flash the lower courses of shingles to keep melting snow from working into the walls. Gutters and downspouts are particularly desirable for houses without overhanging eaves. Flash horizontal wood surfaces or projections, including windows and doors, with a noncorroding metal.

In general, architectural frills or novel forms of construction should be studied carefully to determine whether they will provide entrance points or pockets in which moisture will remain long enough to let decay get started. Lumber takes water most readily through cut ends, as in joints.

## Naturally Decay-Resistant Wood

The sapwood of all species of trees is susceptible to decay. The heartwood of most species, usually recognizable by its redder or darker color, is more durable. In Douglas fir, southern pine, and white oak, the heartwood is classed as moderately decay-resistant. In tidewater red cypress, in most cedars, and in redwood, the heartwood is highly resistant to decay and can even be used in contact with soil and semipermanent construction if there is no sapwood attached. However, even these woods do not have the decay resistance of wood fully impregnated with an effective preservative.

The highly durable hardwoods, such as black walnut, catalpa, Osage orange, and the better varieties of black locust, are too hard or too scarce for general use in construction.

Heartwood of resistant species is increasingly difficult to obtain and cannot be relied on as the principal means of protection from decay in most house construction. Where preservative-treated lumber is not available for use, it is good practice to pick out the pieces containing only heartwood for use in sills, porches, outside steps, and the lowest siding boards.

## Paint and Preservatives

Painting is not a substitute for good construction and good maintenance, nor is paint a preservative. However, it helps to prevent decay by protecting wood from intermittent wetting—especially if it is applied to ends and edges as well as to exposed faces and if it is maintained to allow the fewest possible cracks at joints. When applied to wood that is not seasoned, however, paint may favor decay by hindering further drying.

To prevent decay, use treated wood for any members that are not likely to be properly protected against excessive moisture, unless heartwood of a highly resistant species is available. Sills or plates, sleepers, joists, beams, and girders in or on concrete and exposed porches and steps are the members for which thorough preservative treatment can be easily justified.

To be fully protected, wood must be deeply impregnated with the preservative. This can be done best by treatment under pressure, using (when necessary) preservatives that permit painting. Less efficient but often adequate treatment can be given by so-called vacuum treatment or by heating wood and then soaking it in a cold preservative. For thin or short pieces, cold soaking is sufficient. Wood that is cut and fitted after treatment should be given a soaking or heavy brush treatment of the cut surfaces.

Wood can be given some protection from decay by more superficial treatments with preservatives, although chemicals added by dipping penetrate most woods surprisingly little. Such treatment, while it is not dependable for wood exposed to severe conditions, can considerably increase the service life of wood that will be exposed to rain but will not be in contact with the ground. Including water-repellent materials in the preservative formula makes the treatment more effective, particularly if the wood is to be left unpainted. Painting the wood after treatments of this type increases their effectiveness, especially if water repellents are not added.

It is even possible in some situations to give a somewhat effective treatment to uninfected wood already in place in a building, especially at joints and column ends. Ordinary brushing with preservatives does little, but heavy spraying or otherwise flooding a water-repellent preservative into joint areas can be helpful. Certain greaselike preservatives also are sold for this purpose.

There are difficulties with these superficial treatments. The parts of a building most likely to decay are not always easily reached. If they are covered with a good coating of paint, they will not take treatment. Moreover, a surface thoroughly treated with a solution or grease-like compound containing one of the heavier oils may not take paint for some months. It is much easier and better to treat the wood before it goes into construction, but treated or

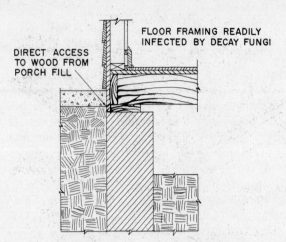

A badly constructed porch with dirt fill can attract the most destructive of the decay fungi.

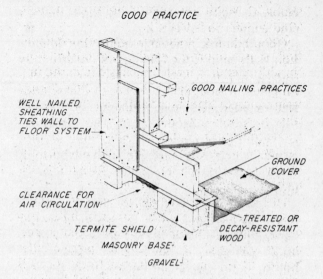

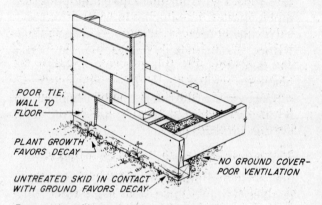

Do not permit wood to come in contact with the soil unless the wood has been properly treated. Shown here are good and poor practices for foundations.

untreated, it should still be protected from excessive moisture.

## SAFEGUARDING WOODWORK CLOSE TO THE GROUND

Older houses built well above the ground are safest from wood decay, but most people prefer modern, low houses. This style, together with the unavoidable use of sapwood from second-growth timber, increases the decay hazard. Sills, joists, floors, and lower walls may suffer heavily from decay fungi that come from the soil. Decay may be hastened by moisture that comes from the soil as vapor and condenses on the cold sills or the outer ends of the joists when the outdoor temperature is low.

### Drainage

Moist building sites should be well drained. The soil surface should slope away from the house, and downspouts should discharge into approved drains or into masonry gutters or splash blocks that lead the water several feet away from the house. Dense shrubbery or vines planted too close to the house can interfere with drainage and air movement and thus promote fungus growth.

### Contact of Wood with Soil

Do not allow wood to be in contact with the soil unless the wood is thoroughly impreg-

nated with a suitable preservative. For the greatest safety to permanent buildings, there should be no wood-soil contact of any kind. Remove all wood forms, grading stakes, and spreader sticks from concrete work under the house, porches, and steps. Wood skirting should have a low concrete base under it, and so should lattice. If a concrete base is not used, then skirting and lattice should be suspended above the soil with a clearance of at least 2 inches. This rule also applies to wood housings around plumbing and water pipes underneath houses. Mineral insulation is preferable to wood housing around pipes that get cold enough to "sweat."

Good building practice requires that foundation walls supporting wood frame construction should extend at least 8 inches above the finish grade, with at least 6 inches of the exterior wall exposed. This means that the bottoms of sills or sleepers would be at least 8 inches above the finish grade. The minimum interior clearance between the ground and the bottoms of joists should be 18 inches; for girders, 12 inches.

Dirt fills under concrete or masonry porch floors frequently provide points of entry for decay fungi. If the dirt under the porch comes up to the level of the sills or joists of the house, these can be protected from contact with the soil by noncorrosive metal flashing or by building the porch as an independent unit separated from the house at all points by an air space 2 or 3 inches in width; this space should be covered at the top. A safe and perhaps easier method is to abandon the use of the dangerous dirt fill and pour a reinforced concrete porch slab. If this is done, leave an opening large enough to allow removal of wood forms and to serve as a permanent access for inspection.

## Contact of Wood with Concrete or Masonry

Embedding wood in concrete near the soil is an invitation to decay. This is especially true of stakes left projecting through the concrete. For slab-on-ground construction, impregnate plates, sleepers, and any other wood in contact with the slab with a preservative, or use naturally durable wood. Treated or naturally durable wood also is desirable for frames and doors of access openings in foundation walls.

Protect wood posts resting on concrete floors from floor moisture by placing them on raised concrete bases or by using treated or naturally durable wood.

Around houses with wood floors and masonry walls, the outside soil grade should be kept below the level of the joists unless the wall is thoroughly moisture-proofed. Joists or girders framed into masonry should have a half-inch air space on each side and at the ends, or the ends should be damp-proofed.

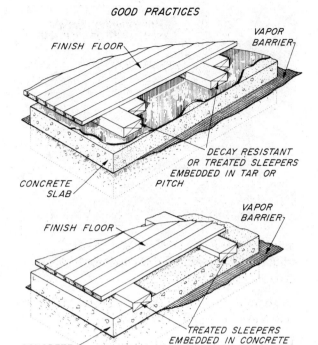

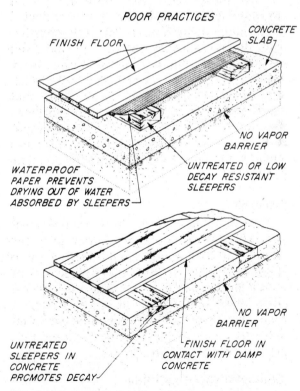

Good and poor practices in wood construction over concrete slabs

In a house with no basement, moisture condensation such as this can be avoided by ventilation or by covering the soil in the crawl space with roll roofing.

USDA Photo

## Ventilation

Under houses without cemented basements, the soil supplies moisture vapor to the air. In winter this may condense on the cold sills and joist ends, just as the moisture of the air condenses on a glass of ice water. This "sweating," if continued, wets the wood to the point where decay fungi can attack it. To avoid this and also to make inspections possible, there should be a crawl space under the house with a clearance of at least 18 inches under the joists.

There are two ways to prevent condensation. One way is to provide cross ventilation for all parts of the crawl space by openings in the foundation or skirting on opposite sides of the building near the corners. For most houses, the formula of 1 square foot of vent opening for each 25 linear feet of wall is sufficient. If the vents have grills in them, count only the area of the actual openings. If the vents have louvers, they should be twice as large. If they have both louvers and 16-mesh screen, they should be three times as large. Insect screen commonly becomes clogged with paint, dirt,

and cobwebs. It is better to use quarter-inch mesh, which keeps out rodents. Keep vents open in winter, and insulate pipes and floors to provide protection from the cold.

It is only on very moist sites that so much ventilation is needed for occupied houses. When houses are not occupied and not heated during the winter, condensation may occur on all floor members instead of being limited to those near the outside.

The second way to prevent condensation is to place a vapor-resistant cover over the ground in the crawl space. This prevents the formation of the moisture vapor that causes the sweating, and makes it possible to use smaller vents or to close most or all of the vents during cold weather without bringing on decay. Smooth-surfaced roll roofing weighing 55 pounds or more per roll of 108 square feet has been used successfully under many houses. Roll out the roofing with a 2-inch lap at the edges; no cementing is needed. Other vapor barrier materials, such as 6-mil polyethylene, also can be used this way.

The use of a soil cover under houses without basements also decreases the likelihood of moisture condensation in attics.

Where the water supply enters the house at a temperature as low as 50°F., there may be enough condensation on concealed pipes in walls and floors to favor decay. In houses with such a supply system, insulate the cold water pipes before they are enclosed. Ventilation cannot fill the need in such cases.

## SAFEGUARDING PARTS OF HOUSES EXPOSED TO RAIN

As previously stated, overhanging roofs and flashing help to protect woodwork. Some decay is to be expected in porches, steps, floors, railings, or pillars exposed to rain. This can be delayed, however.

### Porches and Steps

Construction should be designed to shed rainwater. For example, build railings so that the handrail extends over the tops of the posts or balusters and keeps them from taking rainwater through the ends. Make porch floors slope toward the outside. See that screen

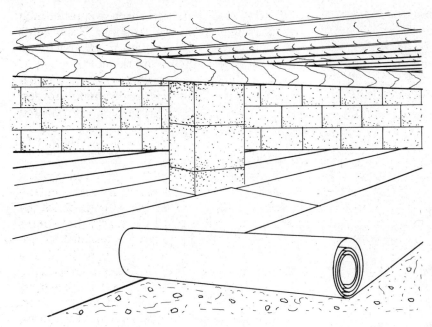

*Roll roofing is used to cover the soil to keep moisture from vaporizing and then condensing on sills and joists.*

frames have openings through the bottom to allow rainwater to escape.

Wood preservatives are especially likely to repay their cost for porches, outside steps, and railings made of wood of low natural durability. There are commercial impregnation treatments available for wood to be painted. When a more thorough treatment is not practicable, immerse lumber in one of the water-repellent preservatives that does not interfere with painting. Keep the wood in the preservative at least three minutes and preferably ten to fifteen minutes or longer. Before painting, allow the treated wood to dry long enough for the solvent to evaporate.

The preservative treatment will have considerable value, provided the wood is dry at the time of treatment and is not put in direct contact with the ground. Where the entire length cannot be immersed, the ends may be dipped and the sides liberally brushed. Always treat the lumber after it is cut and fitted but before it is put in place, so that all ends have the protection. Solutions of pentachlorophenol, 5 percent, containing a water repellent, and of copper naphthenate containing 2 percent of metallic copper, are among the preservatives that have given good results in dipping tests for wood to be used above ground. If the wood is to be painted, mineral spirits or naphtha are good solvents. For wood to be left unpainted, use a heavier solvent such as diesel or No. 2 fuel oil. Many of the compounds are poisonous; some are flammable. Exercise caution in using them, and observe all warnings given on the container label.

If no preservative is used, apply thick paint or white lead to the ends and edges of floorboards before they are put in place to hinder the absorption of water or loss of preservative at the joint. Paint the upper surfaces and edges and ends of floorboards and stair treads, but not the lower surfaces. Protect bases of porch pillars against moisture by using a thick coating of asphalt or white lead on the lower surface; a preservative treatment beforehand is also desirable.

### Windows and Doors

A window sash may discolor or decay, especially in colder climates, where water condenses on the inside of the glass in winter and runs down into the wood. A storm sash is effective in decreasing such condensation. To hinder moisture absorption by the wood, the sash should be primed and back-puttied before

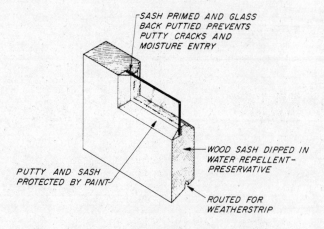

GOOD PRACTICE

SASH PRIMED AND GLASS
BACK PUTTIED PREVENTS
PUTTY CRACKS AND
MOISTURE ENTRY

WOOD SASH DIPPED IN
WATER REPELLENT-
PRESERVATIVE

PUTTY AND SASH
PROTECTED BY PAINT

ROUTED FOR
WEATHERSTRIP

POOR PRACTICE

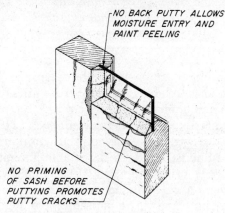

NO BACK PUTTY ALLOWS
MOISTURE ENTRY AND
PAINT PEELING

NO PRIMING
OF SASH BEFORE
PUTTYING PROMOTES
PUTTY CRACKS

*In constructing a window sash, use preventive
methods to avoid moisture entry.*

GOOD PRACTICE

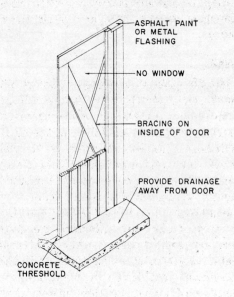

ASPHALT PAINT
OR METAL
FLASHING

NO WINDOW

BRACING ON
INSIDE OF DOOR

PROVIDE DRAINAGE
AWAY FROM DOOR

CONCRETE
THRESHOLD

POOR PRACTICE

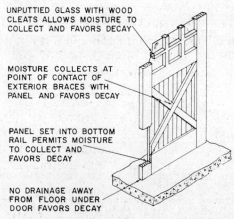

UNPUTTIED GLASS WITH WOOD
CLEATS ALLOWS MOISTURE TO
COLLECT AND FAVORS DECAY

MOISTURE COLLECTS AT
POINT OF CONTACT OF
EXTERIOR BRACES WITH
PANEL AND FAVORS DECAY

PANEL SET INTO BOTTOM
RAIL PERMITS MOISTURE
TO COLLECT AND
FAVORS DECAY

NO DRAINAGE AWAY
FROM FLOOR UNDER
DOOR FAVORS DECAY

*Garage doors should be built to shed water.
Use a preservative treatment to prevent water
from entering the building.*

glazing. Much of the sash and some of the window frames on the market have been dip-treated with a water-repellent preservative that increases their resistance to fungi. The lower ends of window and door screens, if not treated by the manufacturer, can profitably be soaked for a few minutes in a similar solution before painting to get the preservative into the joints. Any surfaces newly exposed when fitting should be given one or two heavy brush coats of the water-repellent preservative.

Garage doors should be built to shed water. Rails, braces, or moldings are best placed on the inner face of the door. On the outside, they trap water between themselves and the vertical members. The use of treated doors or the application of preservative to all contact surfaces in joints, as suggested for porches and steps, is also desirable. Door frames should not extend into the concrete. Any glass in the door should be set in putty, and the wood cleats bedded in putty. Overhead or lateral-sliding doors are less exposed to conditions favoring decay than are outward-swinging doors.

## Walls

Roofs without overhang or gutters allow too much rainwater to run over the siding. Leaks in cornices, gutters, or downspouts can lead to decay in the walls below them. In well-maintained houses, however, frame walls well above the soil line suffer from decay only when there is some unusual combination of factors that permits accumulation of water in the siding or the interior of the wall. Common sources of excessive moisture are green lumber, wet plaster, cold-weather condensation of water vapor in the wall from the interior of the house, rain driven by wind, and excessive running of lawn sprinklers against the house. One of the most important safeguards is to use only dry lumber that is free of fungus stains.

Flashing of noncorroding metal should be used to keep water out of joints that are otherwise difficult to protect. Ornamental drop siding with rounded or slanting lower edges which lead water into the joints is not as safe as the more usual types shaped so that water drips from the lower edge of each board to the face of the siding board below. Siding decay is most frequent in ends that are butted against the trim, for example, at windows, doors, and corners. If the siding ends are under the trim, as is common with drop siding, less moisture gets into the ends and there is less chance for decay.

Some building papers, especially those with a continuous internal layer of asphalt or a shiny asphalt coating, greatly hinder the passage of moisture vapor. In a cold climate such vapor barriers help to keep the wall dry if used on the inner face of the studding. For sheathing paper outside the studding only "breathing" papers should be used. Asphalt-saturated, uncoated papers weighing as much as 15 pounds per 100 square feet may be too impervious for sheathing paper. Insulating material having a vapor-barrier surface should be placed in the wall so that the barrier surface is at the inner (warm) face of the wall.

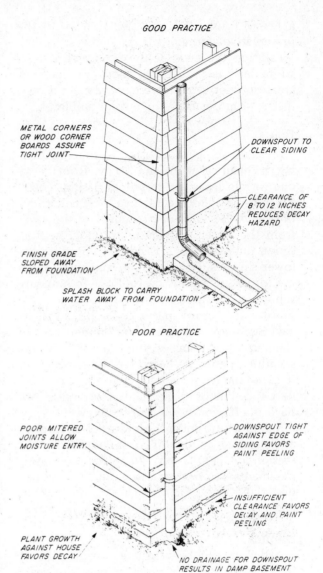

GOOD PRACTICE

METAL CORNERS OR WOOD CORNER BOARDS ASSURE TIGHT JOINT

DOWNSPOUT TO CLEAR SIDING

CLEARANCE OF 8 TO 12 INCHES REDUCES DECAY HAZARD

FINISH GRADE SLOPED AWAY FROM FOUNDATION

SPLASH BLOCK TO CARRY WATER AWAY FROM FOUNDATION

POOR PRACTICE

POOR MITERED JOINTS ALLOW MOISTURE ENTRY

DOWNSPOUT TIGHT AGAINST EDGE OF SIDING FAVORS PAINT PEELING

INSUFFICIENT CLEARANCE FAVORS DECAY AND PAINT PEELING

PLANT GROWTH AGAINST HOUSE FAVORS DECAY

NO DRAINAGE FOR DOWNSPOUT RESULTS IN DAMP BASEMENT

*Correct installation of siding joints and downspouts is important to protect the sides of the building from excess moisture.*

The danger of decay in siding is not great enough to justify the expense of thorough preservative treatment. However, a dip or equivalent treatment of siding is finding increasing favor as a safeguard against decay and for better paint performance. In warm, moist climates, it may be helpful to dip at least the ends of sapwood siding in a water-repellent preservative. In addition, give all surfaces of the siding boards near the bottom of the wall a heavy brush or spray treatment with the preservative before painting.

Painting the ends of the siding with thick white lead is probably a good practice. For greatest safety, the lowest board should be 6 inches or more above the outside soil level.

## Roofs

In time, shingles deteriorate from weathering, mechanical wear, and decay. Roof decay due to rain leaks and improper flashing sometimes is troublesome in sheathing and fascia boards. Leaks may also occur near the eaves from the water that backs up under melting show, unless flashing is carried up under the lower shingles. Cold-weather condensation on the lower surface of the roof due to moisture vapor that comes from living quarters or from moist soil in crawl spaces also can lead to decay. Such condensation is rare under roofs of slate or wood shingles unless a nonbreathing sheathing paper has been used in the roof, but it is common under asphalt roofing, particularly if ceiling or roof insulation used does not have an efficient vapor barrier below it.

Soil moisture under the house can be stopped at its source by the soil cover described in the section on ventilation. Flues for ventilating basements or crawl spaces should never open under the roof. Vapor-barrier paint on walls and ceilings of the living quarters, or vapor-barrier paper or foil just above the ceiling is helpful.

Attics should be ventilated, with vents at opposite sides and preferably near the peak. These vents should have a total unobstructed area of $1/300$ of the ceiling area. Multiply the vent area by 1.25 if the vents are covered by eighth-inch mesh screen, or by 2.25 if louvers are also added. In addition to ventilation, flat roofs particularly need protection by properly placed vapor barriers because it is often difficult to provide free air movement under all parts of such roofs.

## Plywood and Fiberboard

Plywood and the various fiberboards used in recent construction generally require the same precautions as lumber. Resin flues used in exterior-grade plywood are fungus-resistant but do not penetrate the wood enough to make it fungus-proof. With either fiberboard or plywood, joint construction should be carefully designed to prevent the entrance of rainwater. On edges of exposed plywood, use a heavy coat of thick white-lead paint or other moisture-resistant coating. Avoid or flash horizontal joints or water tables on outside walls because they often let rainwater in behind them. Use exterior grades of plywood not only in places exposed to rain but also preferably for roof sheathing or over a crawl space.

When heat insulation is used, the likelihood of moisture condensation and decay in the structure may be increased. To counteract this, place a vapor barrier between the insulating material and the inside of the house. Tight vapor barriers on the outer (cold) surface of the insulation increase the chance of decay.

## REPAIR AND MAINTENANCE

A building frequently requires correction for shortcomings in the original construction. But even if the builder's job has been well done in every respect, inspection and continued care are needed. No house will stand neglect for long. Rust stains around nailheads, peeling and blistering of paint, paint discoloration at joints, and swelling and buckling of siding are some of the signs that moisture is not being controlled. Leaks in roofs, gutters, or plumbing and the clogging and overflow of gutters, downspouts, or drains can lead to wood decay.

Cold pipes that "sweat" and moisten adjacent wood for long periods should be insulated. If crawl-space ventilators are closed during the winter, be sure to open them in early spring to lessen the chance of decay. Do not allow soil, trash, firewood, or lumber to pile up against walls or sills. Likewise, do not raise the exterior grade to a level that brings it dangerously close to the wood.

## Stopping Ordinary Decay

If the house has a wood porch or steps, replace obviously decayed boards or pillar bases with treated or naturally durable wood. Localized decay in joints and bases of uprights may be arrested by flooding treatments with water-repellent preservatives. Decay in sash or windowsills often means that there has been too much condensation of moisture on the inside of the glass. If this sweating cannot be decreased by the measures suggested under "Windows and Doors," take the sash out and allow it to stand with the bottom rail submerged in a water-repellent preservative solution. Replacement sash should be factory-treated or should be given a short soak in the same preservative before it is installed or painted. Decay in window or door frames often means that more flashing is needed. If there is decay in siding, follow the recommendations in the section on walls. If cracks open up so that water can run into them, use a caulking gun occasionally.

If the net area of constantly open vents in a crawl space does not meet the requirements explained in the section on ventilation, the sills and ends of the joists, particularly at the north side, should be examined in winter for decay or for visible moisture. The moisture may appear as conspicuous hanging drops or simply as a wet surface. Measures for avoiding decay from excess moisture that cannot be traced to leaks or direct soil contact can be found under "Ventilation."

In midwinter, examine attics (especially insulated attics) that lack the amount of ventilation advised under "Roofs." Look for condensation, frost accumulation, and decay—especially at the eaves level on the north side of the house. If paint failures are especially troublesome on the north wall or if dark stains develop from moisture seeping out from under the siding, moisture condensation in the walls may be your problem. If condensation persists into warm weather, it can cause decay. Attic condensation can be corrected easily by increased ventilation. This, combined with the ventilation or soil cover advised for crawl spaces and with vapor-proofing for the warm faces of walls, should make the walls safe.

## Stopping "Dry Rot"

Decay that is found to extend many feet from the nearest possible source of moisture is likely to be caused by one of the water-conducting fungi. Between two layers of

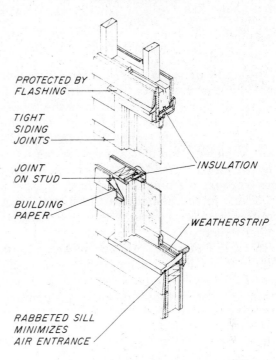

GOOD PRACTICE

PROTECTED BY FLASHING

TIGHT SIDING JOINTS

JOINT ON STUD

BUILDING PAPER

INSULATION

WEATHERSTRIP

RABBETED SILL MINIMIZES AIR ENTRANCE

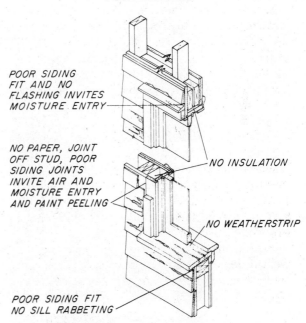

POOR PRACTICE

POOR SIDING FIT AND NO FLASHING INVITES MOISTURE ENTRY

NO PAPER, JOINT OFF STUD, POOR SIDING JOINTS INVITE AIR AND MOISTURE ENTRY AND PAINT PEELING

NO INSULATION

NO WEATHERSTRIP

POOR SIDING FIT NO SILL RABBETING

*Tight joints in the siding at the casing and under the sill of a window or door frame will help prevent rain leakage and air infiltration.*

wood, such as floor and subfloor, these fungi commonly produce rootlike strands thicker and more conspicuous than those previously discussed. The mistaken term "dry rot" is most often associated with these species. Ventilation or vapor barriers may limit their spread but may not stop them entirely.

The treatment needed is to trace the fungus back to its source of moisture, usually the ground, and cut the connection. Often moisture comes up through a brace, frame, concrete form, or grade stake that serves as a bridge to let the fungus travel from moist soil to a joist or sill. Sometimes a joist is in direct contact with a tree stump that has been left under the house.

In other cases, the source from which these fungi obtain moisture may not be so easily located. They sometimes get their moisture from the soil without direct wood contact, through strands of mycelium that grow over the surface of foundation walls or through cracks in masonry.

Use sound, dry wood to replace any that has been made useless by decay. If the sources of moisture for the fungi are entirely eliminated, replace only the wood that has been weakened. When there is any doubt about the moisture-proofing, however, it is safest to remove also the apparently sound wood 2 feet in each direction from the part appreciably decayed and to make replacements with wood that has been thoroughly impregnated with a preservative. This precaution is especially important if the original decay spread rapidly. Before putting the new wood in place, give all adjacent old wood and masonry surfaces a heavy brush treatment with a preservative such as 5 percent pentachlorophenol, or copper naphthenate containing 2 percent copper.

# Roofs 4

The roof, gutters, and downspouts together perform a major job in protecting the house against the deteriorating effects of rain and snowfall. Proper installation and maintenance of these "watersheds" is of crucial importance to the exterior and interior condition of the building.

## ROOF REPAIR

Inspect the roofs of your buildings frequently. Check for breaks, missing shingles, choked gutters, damaged flashing, and defective mortar joints at chimneys, parapets, and coping. Repair defects promptly. Even small defects can result in damage to the sheathing, framing, and interior finish. You can probably repair small defects yourself. Large defects or failures should be repaired by experienced workmen. An inexperienced person may do more harm than good.

### Locating Leaks

As soon as a wet spot appears on a wall or ceiling, inspect the roof to determine the cause. The location of the spot may indicate the trouble. If it is near a chimney or exterior wall, look for defective or narrow flashing or loose mortar joints. On flat roofs, look for choked downspouts or an accumulation of water or snow higher than the flashing. On sloping roofs, look for corroded, loose, or displaced flashing and rotten shingles at valleys and at the junctions of dormers with the roof.

Other frequent causes of leaks are:

1. Holes in the roof covering—generally the cause on plain roofs.
2. Loose or defective flashing around the cupolas and around the plumbing vent pipes.
3. Gutters arranged so that when they are choked they overflow into the house.
4. A ridge of ice along the eaves that backs up melting snow under the shingles.
5. Water leaking from downspouts splashes against a wall and enters through a defect.

### Shingles

Replace missing shingles with the same kind of shingle or a piece of rust-resistant metal. In an emergency, make a temporary repair with metal cut from a tin can. If metal is used, paint it on both sides. Slip it under the shingle in the course above. Be careful not to dislodge sound shingles.

### Metal Roofing

Close small holes in steel or tin roofing with a drop of solder. Solder a patch of the same kind of metal over large holes. If soldering tools are not handy, seal small holes with elastic roofer's cement. Paste a piece of canvas over large holes, using paint as the adhesive. Apply several coats of paint over the patch.

Close small holes in aluminum roofing with a sheet-metal screw and neoprene washer or with an aluminum-pigmented caulking compound. Holes up to $3/8$ inch in diameter can be closed also with cold solder. Holes over $1/2$ inch in diameter should be covered with an aluminum patch. Coat the patch with aluminum-pigmented caulking mastic, and fasten it with sheet-metal screws.

New short sheets may be used to repair large defects in metal roofing. If the defect is near the bottom of the old sheet, remove several fasteners, slip the new sheet under the damaged area, and refasten the old sheet in the same holes. If the defect is near the top, follow the same procedure, but place the new sheet over the damaged area.

### Flashing

Repairs to flashing should be made at the time the roofing is repaired or when inspection shows defects.

Fasten loose flashing securely in place and fill the joint with roofer's cement. If the joint is wide, oakum rolled in roofer's cement may be caulked in the joint.

Replace badly corroded metal in open valleys. Closed valleys are harder to repair. Where leaks occur, try to slip a piece of metal—a square piece folded on the diagonal—up under the shingles. If this cannot be done readily, call in a roofer.

Rake out loose mortar in chimney joints, and repoint the joints with a mixture of one part portland cement, one part lime, and six parts sand.

## NEW ROOFING OVER OLD

When you plan to reroof an old building, consider laying the new covering over the old. This is not always possible or desirable, but there are advantages:

1. The old roofing will provide additional insulation.
2. You can lay the new roofing without exposing the interior of the building or the sheathing to the weather.
3. You avoid the labor, expense, and mess of removing the old covering.

The roof framing must be strong enough to support the additional weight. If your roofing is exceptionally heavy, you may have to brace the rafters, or if they cannot be properly braced, you may have to remove the old covering.

Rigid shingles and metal roofings may be laid over old roll roofing and asphalt shingles if the surface is not puffy or badly wrinkled. Puffy areas should be slit or cut and the old roofing nailed flat. If the new roofing is metal, cover the old roofing with rosin-sized paper (asphalt-saturated felt for aluminum).

Metal roofings may be laid over old wood shingles. Nail 2- by 4-inch nailing strips over the shingles, parallel to the eaves. Fasten the strips to the decking. For lightweight aluminum roofing, space the strips 16 inches on center. End laps of the metal roofing sheets should be over strips. If the new roofing is aluminum, cover nailheads in the strips with aluminum-pigmented mastic or asphalt-saturated felt.

New wood shingles can be laid over old. First, nail flat and secure all curled, badly warped, and loose shingles, and hammer down all protruding nails. Use five-penny nails $1^3/4$ inches long for the new shingles. The old shingles may have been laid on lath or strips. However, in nailing the new shingles, it is not necessary that the nails strike these strips.

*When laying new shingles over old shingles, first cut away 2 to 4 inches of the old shingles along eaves and gables.*

*Second, nail on wood strips to provide a firm nailing base.*

*Third, nail wood strips level with the old shingle surface in the open valleys, then lay new metal valley sheets on top of the wood strips.*

*Fourth, lay a double course of new shingles at the eaves, install the new chimney flashing, and nail strips of bevel siding.*

Many types of roofing are available—asphalt or asbestos-cement shingles, roll roofing, galvanized steel, aluminum, wood shingles, slate, and others. They vary in durability, fire resistance, insulating value, and other properties.

Make your selection carefully, whether you are covering a new building or reroofing an old one. Some important considerations in selecting roofing are roof slope, weight of roofing material, cost, fire resistance, appearance, and location.

## Slope

For each different type of roofing, there is a minimum roof slope using the standard end or side lap. If the slope is less than the minimum, there can be serious damage from leakage.

## Weight

Roofing materials vary in weight. If the roofing is too heavy for the framing, sagging may occur. A roof that sags is unsightly and hard to keep repaired.

## Cost

Roofing materials vary widely in price. Cost in roofing, however, involves more than the cost of the materials. Labor, decking, scaffolding, and other factors make up a large part of the cost.

In selecting roofing from the standpoint of cost, keep these points in mind:

1. Good-quality, long-lived roofing should be used on permanent buildings, even though

## Recommended Weights for Roof Coverings

| Type of roofing | Minimum rise per foot run with ordinary lap (inches) | Approximate weight per square[1] (pounds) |
|---|---|---|
| Aluminum | 4 | 30 |
| Asbestos shingle: | | |
|    American multiple | 5 | 300 |
|    American ranch | 5 | 260 |
| Asbestos, corrugated | 3 | 300 |
| Asphalt shingle: | | |
|    Lockdown | 4 | 290 |
|    3-tab | 4 | 210 |
| Built-up roofing | ½ | 600 |
| Canvas (8 to 12 ounce) | ½ | 25 |
| Galvanized steel: | | |
|    Corrugated | 4 | 100 |
|    V-crimp | 2½ | 100 |
| Roll roofing: | | |
|    Regular (2- to 4-inch lap) | 4 | 100 |
|    Selvage edge (17- to 19-inch lap) | 1 | 140 |
| Slate | 6 | 800 |
| Tin: | | |
|    Standing seam | 3 | 75 |
|    Flat seam | ½ | 75 |
| Wood shingles | 6 | 200 |

[1] The different types of roofing vary in weight per square according to the weight or thickness of the roofing material itself.

the first cost is high. If maintenance, repair, and replacement are considered, low-quality roofing can be more expensive in the long run.

2. Long-lived roofing is warranted when the cost of applying the roofing is high in comparison with the cost of the materials, or when access to the roof is hazardous.

3. Near a supply center, good-quality roofing may be available at lower-than-normal cost. For example, slate, one of the most durable roofing materials, usually is one of the most expensive. However, near a quarry, the price may be comparable with that of lower-quality, less-durable roofing.

### Fire Resistance

Roofing materials vary in fire resistance. Slate, asbestos-cement shingles, and metal roofings are the most fire resistant. Others, such as asphalt shingles and roll roofing, provide satisfactory protection if they are of good quality and are kept in good condition.

Your house and other important buildings on your property should have a fire-resistant roof covering, if possible. Buildings closely grouped together—less than 150 feet apart—also should have fire-resistant coverings. If one catches fire, the danger of fire from flying sparks to the other buildings will be minimized.

### Location

Along seacoasts the air is saturated with salt; around industrial works it may be polluted with fumes. The salt and fumes may corrode galvanized or aluminum roofings and shorten their life. Steel roofing, even though galvanized, is particularly susceptible to such corrosion. If used, it must be kept well painted.

For maximum service and protection, install the roofing properly and keep it in good repair. Improper installation and poor maintenance can result in leaks or other trouble and can shorten the life of the roofing.

### ESTIMATING ROOFING NEEDS

After having selected the type of roofing, you will want to determine the amount of roofing material needed. This should be done by someone experienced in estimating roofing. The following is offered as a guide.

Roofing materials are commonly sold by the square, which is 100 square feet. The number of squares needed will be determined by the area of the roof in square feet.

Extra material is required for overhang at eaves and gables and for fitting around chimneys, dormers, and valleys. Include this in your estimate. Allow also for waste.

### WOOD SHINGLES

Wood shingles, if they are of a durable species and properly laid, make a satisfactory, attractive, and well-insulated roof. Different grades of shingles are on the market. The best ones are edge-grained and all heartwood (No. 1 grade). Shingles in all grades below No. 1 are flat-grained or contain varying amounts of sapwood.

No. 1 grade shingles are recommended for permanent roofs—especially for house roofs. The lower grades of shingles are not economical for permanent construction, but are suitable for temporary roofs and for sidewalls.

No. 1 grade southern cypress, redwood, and cedar shingles are the most decay resistant.

Wood shingles are made in lengths of 16, 18, and 24 inches. Ordinarily they come in random widths from $2^1/_2$ to 14 inches. You can get shingles of uniform width—5 or 6 inches—but they are generally used for decorative effects on roof and sidewalls.

### Deck

In warm, humid climates, wood shingles are commonly nailed to slats to permit ventilation of the underside. A slat roof is light in weight and low in cost. The slats may be 1-inch by 4-inch strips, spaced, center to center, a distance equal to the length of shingle exposed to the weather.

In cold climates, the shingles are usually laid over tight sheathing covered with rosin-sized paper. Slats with insulation board under them are sometimes used.

### Method

One-fourth pitch is the minimum slope recommended for wood shingles. If the slope is

*Wood shingles are nailed over slats
to permit ventilation to the underside.*

*When you finish hips and ridges Boston-style,
the shingles are alternately lapped,
fitted, and blind-nailed.*

much less than one-fourth pitch, it will be hard to keep the roof watertight.

On roofs of one-fourth pitch or steeper, lay the shingles as follows to provide a three-ply roof:

| Shingle length (inches) | Length exposed to weather (inches) |
|---|---|
| 16 | 5 |
| 18 | 5½ |
| 24 | 7½ |

On roofs of less than one-fourth pitch, lay the shingles as follows to provide a four-ply roof:

| Shingle length (inches) | Length exposed to weather (inches) |
|---|---|
| 16 | 3¾ |
| 18 | 4¼ |
| 24 | 5¾ |

Low-grade flat-grained shingles should be laid with the "bark" side exposed (the side that was nearest the bark in the tree). They will weather better and be less likely to turn up at the butt or to become waterlogged.

Split any shingles that are more than 8 inches in width; atmospheric changes can crack wide shingles.

Double the shingles at all eaves and extend them about an inch beyond the edge.

Space dry shingles ¼ inch apart, and green or wet ones ⅛ inch, to allow for swelling in damp weather.

Fasten each shingle with two nails, one on each side, 1 to 2 inches above the butt line of the next course and not more than ¾ inch from the edge. Never nail in the middle because the shingle may split. Use three-penny rust-resistant nails for 16- and 18-inch shingles and four-penny nails for 24-inch shingles. Joints should be broken at least 1½ inches and all nails should be covered.

Check the coursing as the work progresses. The shingle rows must be kept parallel to the eaves to avoid uneven exposure of the last few courses. Hips and ridges may be finished Boston-style.

### Flashing

Painted sheet iron or "tin" is frequently used for flashing with wood shingles. However, more durable material, such as 26- or

24-gauge galvanized metal of the highest quality of heavily coated IX flashing tin, is recommended.

### Staining

Stains rich in coal-tar creosote have much more preservative value than those containing little or no coal-tar creosote. However, shingles treated with such stains cannot be satisfactorily painted; the creosote will bleed through paint even after several years' exposure. Shingles treated with stains containing little or no coal-tar creosote can be painted after short exposure to the weather.

Dipping is the best method of staining a shingle. Dip the shingle to within 3 inches of the tapered end. Brush coats may be applied for additional protection after several years' exposure.

## SLATE SHINGLES

Slate shingles make an attractive, durable, and fire-resistant roof covering. They are available in different grades and in various colors. The best slates have a metallic appearance, do not absorb water, and are very strong. Commercial slates range in size from 6 by 10 to 14 by 24 inches. The more commonly used sizes are 8 by 16, 9 by 12, and 9 by 18 inches.

Some dark slates fade to a lighter gray on exposure. This change in color is not always uniform and the roof may become unattractive. Certain green slates may become buff or brown after a few months' exposure. This change is sometimes considered desirable and it has no effect on the quality of the slate.

Slates are very heavy roofing material—700 to 900 pounds per square—and require strong roof framing.

Slate roofs are commonly installed by roofing contractors.

## ASBESTOS-CEMENT SHINGLES

Asbestos-cement shingles are made of asbestos fiber and portland cement. They are strong, durable, and fire resistant. They are available in a wide variety of colors and surface textures—including their natural color, which is similar to that of portland cement. There is no standard by which to judge the merits of the many variations, and if you plan to use these shingles, select a type that has given good service in your locality.

Asbestos-cement shingles may be classed according to shape and method of application as follows:

1. American-method individual shingles are 8 inches wide and 16 inches long. They are laid like wood shingles and weigh about 350 pounds per square.
2. American multiple shingles usually come in strips 24 to 30 inches long and 12 to 15 inches high. They weigh about 300 pounds per square. When laid, they give the appearance of smaller individual shingles.
3. Side-lap or Dutch-lap shingles are approximately 16 by 16 inches and weigh 265 to 290 pounds per square. They are laid with one-third or one-fourth side and top lap. One-third lap makes a tighter and more attractive roof. One-fourth lap makes a lighter-weight and lower-cost roof.
4. American ranch shingles are 24 by 12 inches and weigh 250 to 260 pounds per square. They are usually laid with one-sixth side lap (20 inches exposed) and one-fourth top lap (9 inches exposed).

Detailed instructions for laying asbestos-cement shingles may be obtained from manufacturers or dealers.

USDA Photo

*American-method individual shingles*

*American multiple shingles*

*Side-lap or Dutch-lap shingles*

*American ranch shingles*

*When laying corrugated asbestos-cement sheets, overlap the sides and ends.*

## ASBESTOS-CEMENT SHEETS

Corrugated asbestos-cement sheets are available for covering roofs consisting of sheathing strips, or purlins, on top of rafters. The sheets are 42 inches wide, 3 to 11 feet long, and $3/8$ or $1/4$ inch thick. The sheets are corrugated at 4.2-inch intervals.

### Deck

Sheets $3/8$ inch thick may be laid on purlins spaced 45 to 54 inches on center. Sheets $1/4$ inch thick may be laid on purlins spaced 30 to 42 inches on center. The exact spacing of the purlins required in each case will depend on expected snow loads.

### Method

The sheets should be laid with a side lap of one corrugation and a minimum end lap of 6 inches. Trim the corners of the sheets to permit continuous lap.

Fasten the sheets to wood purlins with 3-inch ring-shank nails. Fasten them to metal purlins with special fasteners available commercially.

Apply asphalt mastic on each side of the ridge. Set a gasket material on the mastic. Then cover the ridge with a semicircular ridge cap.

## BITUMINOUS ROOFING

Bituminous roofing, in one of many forms, is widely used on farm buildings. Bituminous roofing materials divide into four general classes—lightweight felts, roll roofing, asphalt shingles, and built-up roofing. These roofing materials have a felt base made of rag felt or asbestos felt. Asbestos-felt roofing is more fire resistant than the rag-felt roofing.

### Lightweight Felts

Lightweight asphalt-saturated or tar-saturated felts are used (1) under shingles or other roofing materials, (2) for built-up roofing, and (3) to cover low-cost buildings such as sheds. They serve only as a very temporary roof covering, however, because they are easily torn by the wind.

### Roll Roofing

Roll roofing, of good quality and properly laid, is a suitable covering that has a low initial cost. The roofing, which is also known as prepared, ready, and composition roofing, is composed of asphalt-saturated felt coated with asphalt. It is available in different grades or thicknesses. The heavier grades generally prove more satisfactory and give longer service.

Three forms of roll roofing are available:

1. Mineral-surfaced roofing is coated with mineral granules (ceramic-coated rock or crushed slate) on the weather side and dusted with talc or mica on the underside. It comes in a variety of colors—the color of the granules determines the color of the roofing.
2. Smooth-surfaced roofing is not coated; both sides are dusted with talc or mica. It comes in one color only.
3. Selvage-edge or wide-selvage roofing is coated with asphalt and mineral granules to 1 inch from the middle of the roll. The remainder is not coated with mineral granules, but there should be 2 or 3 inches of asphalt coating extending beyond the mineral granules for weather resistance where two strips of the roofing join. Because it provides two-ply coverage, selvage-edge roofing is more durable and more wind resistant than the other kinds of roll roofing and can be used on lower-pitched roofs. If you buy this roofing, be sure that it is made for use with cold cement and that the cement and the roofing are made by the same manufacturer.

*Deck:* Roll roofing—mineral surfaced, smooth surfaced, and selvage edge—should be laid on tight sheathing.

*Method:* Roll roofing is usually laid with the sheets stretched parallel to the eaves. It can also be laid with the sheets stretched along the slope. If the latter is done, fasten wood battens or metal strips over the long laps for more protection against tearing by the wind.

For mineral-surfaced roofing, lap the strips 2 or 3 inches at the side or edge. Lap the ends of adjoining strips 4 to 6 inches. Use large-headed galvanized nails to fasten the roofing. Space them 2 to 3 inches apart. If a nail goes into a crack between boards, pull it out and patch the hole in the roofing. Tin caps are not recommended. They corrode quickly and leave the nailhead protruding, which makes it easy for the wind to tear off the roofing.

Smooth-surfaced roofing can be laid in the same way as mineral-surfaced roofing, however, the blind-nailing method is recommended. Increase the side lap to 4 inches and the end lap to 6 inches. Nail the underlying edges through tin or fiber disks on 6-inch centers. Cement the overlying edges with hot asphalt or special blind-nailing cement. Step down firmly on these edges to make them stick.

When selvage-edge roofing is laid, be sure that no gap is left between the coated parts of adjoining strips. Sunlight will deteriorate any exposed, unprotected part of the roofing.

Roll roofing is usually fastened at eaves and gables by nailing into the edge of the sheathing. A better method involves the use of battens. Use barbed or cement-coated nails to fasten the battens.

*Flashing:* Flashing should be of the same material as the roofing and in two thicknesses. Rust-resistant metal chimney flashing should be used at chimneys with all but the cheapest roofing. Chimney flashing should be wedged and caulked into the mortar joints.

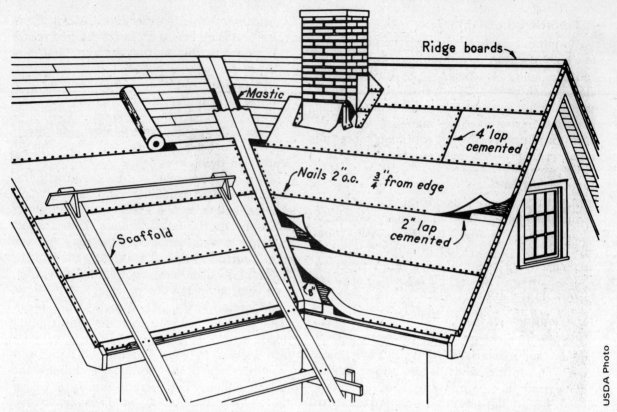

Roll roofing can be laid with the sheets parallel to the eaves, as shown here, or laid with the sheets stretched along the slope.

USDA Photo

## Asphalt Shingles

Asphalt shingles, also called composition shingles, are widely used for roof covering, because of their moderate cost, light weight, and durability. The shingles are composed of asphalt-saturated felt coated with asphalt and are surfaced with mineral granules on the weather side. They are available as single shingles or in strips of several units, and in a wide variety of colors and patterns.

Asphalt shingles are semirigid and susceptible to damage by the wind. Cheap shingles or shingles laid with too much surface exposed may curl badly after weathering. Some asphalt shingles are made so that they can be locked down or interlocked when laid. Strip shingles are available with a self-sealing compound on the tabs. Use one of these types in windy locations.

Strip shingles require less labor to apply than individual shingles. The three-tab strip shingle is one that is commonly used. It is 36 inches long and 12 inches high, and has cutouts 5 inches deep and $3/8$ inch wide. These cutouts produce the appearance of individual shingles.

Detailed directions for laying asphalt shingles normally are included with the shingles when purchased.

## Built-up Roofing

Built-up roofing consists of several layers of lightweight felt, lapped and cemented together with a bituminous material and covered with a layer of small-sized gravel or slag. The roofing is long-lived and low in cost. It has high fire resistance, although it will burn freely once ignited.

The roofing may be used on roofs sloping $1/2$ inch to 3 inches per foot. On greater slopes, it may slip in hot weather and the gravel may not stay in place. On lesser slopes, the uneven surface may prevent proper drainage.

*Different stages are shown in laying asphalt shingles: roof sheathing, felt underlay, and shingles.*

Built-up roofs may be three-, four-, or five-ply, according to the number of layers of felt. A five-ply roof, if laid by skilled workmen in accordance with the manufacturer's specifications, should last twenty years or more.

Built-up roofs are usually installed by contractors who have the necessary equipment and experience.

## METAL ROOFING

Metal roofings include tin, galvanized steel, aluminum, copper, and zinc. (Copper and zinc are not used much because of their high cost. They are laid like tin roofing.) Metal roofings are lightweight and fire resistant. Those laid with locked or soldered joints can be used on low-pitched roofs with little danger of leakage.

Metal roofings have little insulating value. Insulating materials may be needed under them. Proper grounding is required for protection against lightning.

### Tin

So-called tin roofing is actually soft steel or wrought iron coated with a mixture of lead and tin. The material is more properly known as terne metal. A tin roof of good material, properly laid and kept well painted, may last 40 to 50 years.

The roofing is available in strips 50 to 100 feet long and 14, 20, 24, and 28 inches wide. These strips come in rolls for easy handling.

The roofing is made in two thicknesses, IC and IX; IX is the heavier. It is available with a lead-tin coating of 8, 20, or 40 pounds per 436 square feet. Durability of the roofing depends on the thickness of the coating rather than on the thickness of the metal.

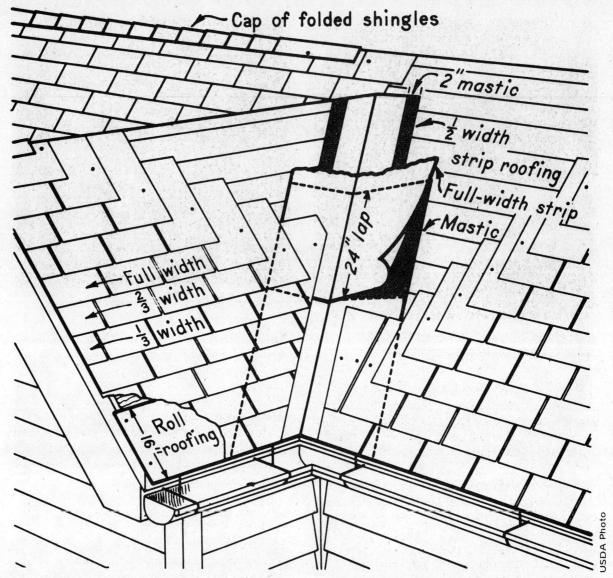

Cap of folded shingles

2" mastic

½ width strip roofing

Full-width strip

Mastic

24" lap

Full width

⅔ width

⅓ width

Roll roofing

⅙

USDA Photo

*In the installation of ordinary asphalt shingles, the valley construction, shown here, will generally apply to all types of shingles.*

Special sheet-metal tools are required to lay tin roofing. If you are not experienced in laying the roofing, it may be advisable to have professional roofers do the work.

*Deck:* Tin roofing should be laid on tight sheathing. Tongue-and-groove boards are recommended. The boards should be well seasoned and of uniform thickness. The deck can be covered with rosin-sized or other tar-free sheathing paper to deaden the noise of wind and rain on the roof.

*Method:* If the roof slope is 3 inches or more per foot, a standing-seam roof should be laid. If the slope is less than 3 inches per foot, a flat-seam roof should be laid.

The cleats of a standing-seam roof should be of the same material as the roofing and should be spaced 8 to 12 inches apart. Fasten them securely to the sheathing. The finished seam should be straight, rounded neatly at the top edge, and stand 1 inch above the roof surface. Standing seams are not soldered.

*Roofing shingles being nailed into place where the two sections of the house are joined*

USDA Photo

Jim Walter Corporation

*A completed roof of asphalt shingles*

A flat-seam roof is laid in the same general way as a standing-seam roof, except that the seams are formed differently and are flattened on the roof. Flat seams should be soldered to make them watertight.

## Galvanized Steel

Galvanized steel roofing is an economical and durable roofing if good materials are used and the roof is properly cared for. Roofing made of alloy steel is more rust resistant than that made of plain steel, but durability depends chiefly on the protective zinc coating. Heavily galvanized roofing gives long service without painting. Lightly galvanized roofing must be kept well painted after it begins to rust.

Roofing with a guaranteed minimum coating of 2 ounces of zinc per square foot is on the market under a special "seal of quality." This is a heavy coating, and the roofing will last a long time under normal conditions. For maximum service, however, it will need painting eventually.

Galvanized steel roofing comes in different thicknesses, indicated by gauge number. The lower the gauge number, the heavier the metal.

Styles of galvanized steel roofing commonly used are V-crimp sheets, corrugated sheets, and trapezoidal configurations of several shapes.

V-crimp sheets are made to cover 24 or 30 inches, allowing for side lap, and they are 6 to 12 feet long. They come with two, three, or five V-crimps. The five-crimp sheets provide a more watertight roof because they are laid with a side lap of two crimps.

Corrugated sheets are 26 inches wide with $1\frac{1}{2}$-inch corrugations, and $27\frac{1}{2}$ inches wide with $2\frac{1}{2}$-inch corrugations. Both widths give 24-inch coverage, allowing for side lap. They are available in lengths of 6 to 32 feet.

Trapezoidal sheets are the strongest of the three styles and are available in the same widths, lengths, and thicknesses as the other two. Special sheets may cover 48 inches in width.

Following are installation details for sheet steel. Additional installation details may be obtained from manufacturers.

*Deck:* Corrugated and trapezoidal sheets may be laid on (1) tight sheathing; (2) 1-inch by 4-inch or 1-inch by 6-inch roofing slats, spaced 2 feet apart, on top of rafters, spaced 2 feet on center; (3) 2-inch by 4-inch purlins on top of rafters; or (4) rafters with 2-inch by 4-inch headers cut between them.

V-crimp sheets should be laid on tight sheathing. Tight sheathing under either type may be covered with rosin-sized sheathing paper.

*Method:* Corrugated sheets are laid with a side lap of $1\frac{1}{2}$ corrugations. End lap is 9 inches if the roof slope is 4 inches per foot, and 6 inches if the slope is more than 6 inches per foot. All laps should be made over supports.

Fasten the sheets at all laps and intermediate supports. Nail down through the tops of the corrugation. Space the nails about 8 inches apart. Screw-type or ring-shank nails are recommended. They should be long enough to fully penetrate the sheathing. The nails should have weather-protected heads, or neoprene washers should be used under the heads.

V-crimp sheets with 2 or 3 crimps should be laid with a side lap of 1 crimp. Those with 5 crimps should be laid with a side lap of 2 crimps. End lap and nailing is the same as corrugated sheets.

*Flashing:* Flashings at hips, valleys, eaves, and chimneys should be of galvanized steel. Open valleys should be used; they should be lined with galvanized steel one or two gauges heavier than the roofing. Special valley sheets are available. Special ridge rolls, joints, and flashings for use at hips, eaves, and chimneys are available and will aid in making a tighter roof.

*Painting:* Galvanized steel roofing should weather for at least a year before it is painted. Clean the roof thoroughly before you paint. Remove rusted spots with a wire brush. Remove any loose nails and renail. Do not paint unless the roof is absolutely dry. The best time is in warm, dry weather. When painting is needed, the proper application of a good zinc-base paint will extend the life of the roof considerably.

## Aluminum

Good grades of aluminum are highly corrosion resistant, require no painting, and require little maintenance. Aluminum reflects a little more heat than steel. Reflection of the hot summer sun's heat keeps the interior of the building cooler.

Two styles of aluminum roofing that are commonly used on buildings are V-crimp sheets and corrugated sheets.

V-crimp sheets are made 26 inches wide with five crimps and about 50 inches wide with eight crimps. These widths provide 24- and 48-inch coverage respectively, allowing for side lap. The sheets are available 6 to 32 feet long and .019 inch and .024 inch thick with smooth or embossed finishes.

Corrugated sheets with either $1\frac{1}{4}$-inch or $2\frac{1}{2}$-inch corrugations are available in the same widths, lengths, and thicknesses as the V-crimp sheets.

Following are installation details for the corrugated sheets and V-crimp sheets. Additional details may be obtained from manufacturers.

*Deck:* Corrugated sheets can be laid on tight sheathing, on 1-inch by 6-inch boards spaced 12 inches on center, or on 2-inch by 4-inch purlins spaced a maximum of 24 inches on center. Spacing of the purlins depends on the weight of the sheets and varies with corrugation size and thickness of sheet.

V-crimp sheets can be laid on tight sheathing or sheathing boards spaced up to 6 inches apart.

Tight sheathing under either type should be covered with 15-pound or heavier asphalt-saturated felt. Lay the felt in horizontal courses, starting at the eaves, and lap the courses a minimum of 3 inches.

The roofing should not touch other kinds of metal. Cover steel nailheads in the sheathing (if it is not covered with asphalt felt) with asphalt-saturated felt or aluminum mastic. If metal purlins, other than aluminum ones, are used, coat them with aluminum-pigmented asphalt.

*Method:* Corrugated sheets with $2\frac{1}{2}$-inch corrugations are laid with a side lap of $1\frac{1}{2}$ corrugations. Sheets with $1\frac{1}{4}$-inch corrugations are laid with a side lap of $2\frac{1}{2}$ corrugations. Side laps should be away from the prevailing winds. End lap should be 6 inches or more. At the eaves, extend the sheets 2 inches beyond the edge of the deck to form a drip edge. Fasten the sheets by nailing through the tops of the corrugations. Use aluminum nails, with neoprene washers under the heads, long enough to fully penetrate the sheathing.

V-crimp sheets should be laid with a side lap of two crimps. End lap is 6 inches or more. Fasten the sheets by nailing down through the tops of the V-crimps. Use aluminum nails with neoprene washers under the heads.

*Flashing:* Aluminum flashing .024 inch thick should be used. Special ridge rolls, joints, and flashings are available for use at hips, eaves, side and end walls, valleys, and chimneys.

## FLASHING

Install flashing—strips of metal or other material—in valleys between intersecting roof surfaces and where the roof joins chimneys and other vertical surfaces to make roof watertight.

Sheet metal—copper, aluminum, galvanized steel, or terne metal—is used for flashing with most types of roofing. Roll roofing or felt is used with bituminous roofings.

Special flashing materials are available. One type is a steel sheet protected on both sides with baked-on coating or bonded asphalt-saturated fabric. Another type is a double layer of bituminous felt reinforced with cotton or steel-wire mesh.

### Painting the Flashing

Zinc, lead, and aluminum flashings are not ordinarily painted. Copper is sometimes painted to prevent the staining of other surfaces, but paint will not last long on untreated copper. Before painting, wash the surface of the

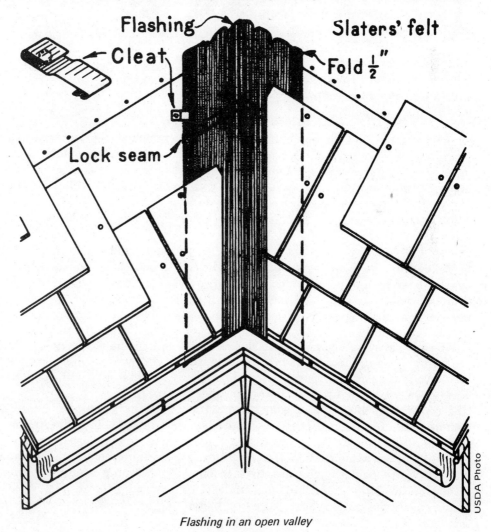

*Flashing in an open valley*

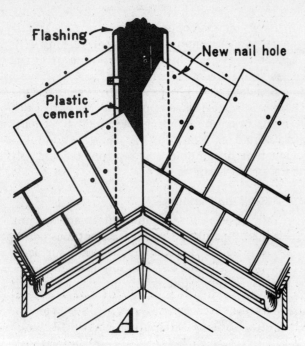
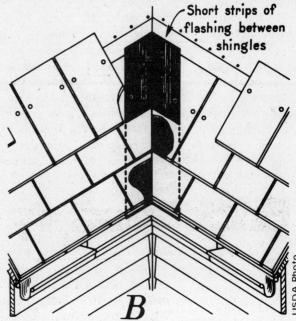

*Flashing in a closed valley: A, long metal
strip under shingles; B, short pieces
of metal intermembered with shingles*

copper with a solution of $1/2$ gallon of luke-warm water, 4 ounces of copper sulfate, and $1/8$ ounce of nitric acid. (Mix the solution in a glass container.) Wash the surface again with water to remove all traces of the acid, and allow it to dry.

### Valley Flashing

Valleys may be open or closed. Open valleys should be at least 4 inches wide at the top and should widen out about $1/8$ inch per foot of length. Use flashing strips at least 20 inches wide.

When a valley is between roof surfaces of different areas or slopes, provide a baffle rib to prevent the larger or faster-descending volume of water from forcing its way up under the roofing on the opposite side. The baffle can be in the form of a V-crimp along the center line of the valley.

There are two methods of flashing closed valleys where rigid shingles are used. In one, a continuous strip of metal is laid under the shingles. In the other, short pieces of metal are built in as the shingles are laid. If a pre-punched nailhole in a slate or asbestos shingle falls over the metal flashing, provide a new hole. Each shingle should be fastened with two nails located outside the metal.

### Vertical Flashing

Flashing at vertical surfaces, such as chimneys and walls, must extend up at least 6 inches and be counterflashed with cap flashing. The two flashings should not be fastened together rigidly.

With a chimney located on the ridge, the cap flashing should be built into the joints when the masonry is laid. This should be folded down at least 4 inches over the base flashing that is installed at the same time as the roofing.

With a chimney located on the slope, the saddle behind the chimney diverts water coming down the slope and prevents ice from forming behind the chimney.

Flashing around plumbing vents extending through the roof must be installed so that the pipe can settle or expand without causing leaks.

# 5
# Brick Masonry

Brick masonry is masonry construction in which bricks of baked clay or shale of uniform size are laid in courses with mortar joints to form walls of virtually unlimited length and height. Brick walls require less frequent maintenance than most exterior walls, but certain failures are not uncommon. Exteriors should be inspected quarterly for structural cracks, open mortar joints, settlement, efflorescence, stains, and deterioration of paint or other surface coverings.

## DEFECTIVE MORTAR JOINTS

The most common fault found in brick and block walls is defective mortar joints. Defective mortar joints can be corrected by repointing, following these procedures:

1. Cut out cracked and open mortar joints to a depth of at least $1/2$ inch. (Cutting can be done by hand, but if large areas are involved, it is usually cheaper to use power tools.) Take care not to damage brickwork during the cutting process.
2. Remove all dust and loose material with brushes, compressed air, or a water jet. If water is used, no further wetting of the joints may be needed unless the work is delayed.
3. Repair the joints by tuck-pointing.
4. Use mortar of about the same density as the original mortar, if that can be determined; otherwise, use a prehydrated mortar mix in the following proportions by volume: one part of portland cement, one part of lime putty or hydrated lime, and six parts of sand.
5. Be sure the joints are damp, and then apply the mortar, working it tightly into the joints in thin layers.
6. Tool the joints to smooth, compact, concave surfaces.

## EFFLORESCENCE

Another problem easily detected during a routine inspection is efflorescence, which usually appears as a light powder or crystallization. It is caused by water-soluble salts deposited as water evaporates from the mortar or the bricks. Aside from the fact that it is unattractive, efflorescence may indicate that moisture has penetrated the wall to an extent that could cause deterioration of interior wall coverings and finishes. Efflorescence may be removed by vigorous and repeated scrubbing with a stiff fiber or wire brush and clean water. An inspection should be made, however, to determine the source of the stain. If efflorescence appears at the edges and not near the centers of bricks, the mortar is probably at fault. If it appears near the centers of the bricks only, the bricks are at fault. The most immediate remedy to prevent recurrence of efflorescence is to check causes of excessive moisture that contacts the wall, such as defective flashings, gutters, downspouts, copings, and mortar joints.

## CRACKS

Cracks may be caused by foundation settlement, excessive floor loading, expansion and contraction in structural members, or poor materials and poor workmanship in the original construction. The types of cracks encountered include horizontal movement cracks, vertical and diagonal movement cracks, and shrinkage cracks. An engineering investigation should govern the nature and extent of major repairs.

Horizontal movement cracks are usually long, wide cracks in the mortar joints that occur along the floor or roof line or along the line of lintels over windows and doors. Where these cracks turn the corner of a building,

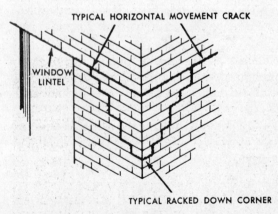

A horizontal movement crack and racked down corner

they frequently "rack down," as discussed below.

Vertical and diagonal movement cracks generally occur near the ends or offsets of buildings. They may also be found extending from a window sill to the lintel of a door or window on a lower floor. They vary from $1/8$ to $3/8$ of an inch in width and follow the mortar joints, but in some instances they may break through the bricks.

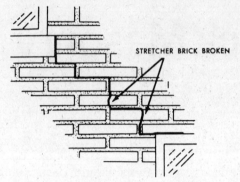

A diagonal movement crack extending from a window sill

Shrinkage cracks are the fine hairline cracks that are found in mortar as well as in concrete walls. The most noticeable ones are those running vertically, but a close examination of a section of wall that leaks may also show them in the horizontal, or bed joint, of the brick.

Racked-down corners occur where the horizontal movement cracks along the side and end of a building meet. Frequently the horizontal crack not only continues around the corner but also forms part of a diagonal crack that takes a downward direction and meets a similar crack from the other side, forming a V. The bricks inside this V are loose and must be reset.

1. First remove all the bricks inside the V, including any bricks that have been broken. This forms irregular sides and helps to hold, or key, the brick in place.
2. After the bricks are removed, clean the sound bricks and obtain as many new matching ones as are necessary to fill the opening. Relay the bricks in mortar up to the horizontal crack running along the side

and end of the building. If all joints are made the same width as the original joints and the mortar tends to match the old mortar, a very presentable job will result. As the bricks are built up, coat the backup bricks with mortar so that the newly laid bricks will be bonded to them.

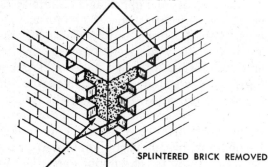

THE HORIZONTAL MOVEMENT CRACK LINE

SPLINTERED BRICK REMOVED

FRACTIONAL TOOTHING BRICK REMOVED

*Remove damaged or loose bricks to be reset.*

*To insert a brick in a space left in a wall, spread a thick bed of mortar.*

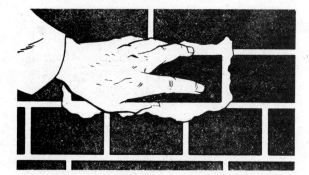

*Shove brick into mortar until mortar is squeezed out.*

3. Partly fill with mortar the top joint that is in line with the horizontal crack. This can be done by pushing the mortar into the joint with a narrow pointing trowel. When about half the depth of the joint is filled, fill the remainder with sealing compound. This system of mortaring only half the top joint holds the bricks but forms a weak plane along the top of the racked down areas. If movement takes place, the mortar joint breaks, but the relaid bricks remain in place. The sealing compound keeps the joint watertight.

## CONDENSATION AND WATERPROOFING

Condensation is frequently mistaken for a leak in a masonry wall. Exterior walls of heated buildings, located in cold climates or in areas subject to cold weather during a portion of the year, may appear to be leaking as a result of water passing through the walls, even though the walls are watertight. In such cases, investigation will usually disclose that when relative humidities within the building are comparatively high, exterior relative humidity is rather low, and exterior temperatures are below the freezing point, moisture vapor tends to travel through the wall from the interior to the exterior. The temperature of the masonry wall is considerably lower than that of the heated interior and the temperature of the exterior face of the wall approaches that of the atmosphere. Water vapor traveling from the interior to the exterior encounters the low temperatures of the brick and condenses in the wall. Damp walls may be the only result, but under certain conditions, freezing and

*With the brick in place, remove excess mortar.*

thawing may occur within the walls, causing cracking and spalling of the masonry and actual leakage.

One way to prevent vapor movement through walls is to install vapor barriers. These are usually plastic or foil sheets that can be part of the insulation or wallboard. Asphalt roll roofing can serve as a vapor barrier in some cases. Some paints or other finishes serve as barriers but are subject to cracking or wear stresses.

Vapor barriers must be placed as near as possible to the warm or inner side of any insulation. This will slow the movement of water vapor through walls and help prevent it from reaching surfaces cold enough for condensation. Plastic sheets are stapled to the inside edge of wall studs and wallboard placed on top. Insulation with attached vapor barriers usually has tabs that overlap and are stapled to the inside edge of the studs. Wallboard with a foil or plastic backing is fastened in place with the foil or plastic facing the studs.

In cool climates vapor barriers are needed in all exterior walls. Vapor barriers should be free of holes and come as close as possible to window and door openings. Any gaps, such as those frequently found around electrical outlet or switch boxes, allow considerable moisture to enter the wall cavity. Caulk around all openings to seal the edges of the vapor barrier.

Another way of controlling moisture is to use a transparent waterproofing compound.

However, the use of transparent waterproofing compounds is justified only when the defects in construction have been corrected and when it is evident that moisture is entering the vertical wall face because of porous materials, not defective joints.

## JOINT FINISHES

Exterior surfaces of mortar joints are finished to make the brickwork more watertight and to improve the appearance. There are several types of joint finishes. When joists are cut flush with the brick and not finished, cracks are immediately apparent between the brick and the mortar. Although these cracks are not deep, they are undesirable and can be eliminated by finishing or tooling the joint. In every case, the mortar joint should be finished before the mortar has hardened appreciably.

The most weathertight joints are the concave and V joints. These joints are made with a special tool after the excess mortar has been removed with the trowel. The tool should be slightly larger than the joint. Force is used to press the mortar tight against the brick on both sides of the mortar joint.

The flush joint is made by keeping the trowel almost parallel to the face of the wall and drawing the point along the joint.

A weather joint, which sheds water easily, is formed by pushing downward on the mortar with the top edge of the trowel.

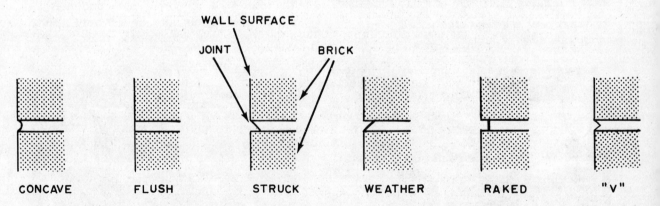

*Types of joint finishes*

# 6
# Concrete

Concrete construction was once largely confined to paving and foundations. Today, it has been developed to the point where both large and small buildings are constructed entirely of concrete. It is used also for driveways, patios, walkways, and walls.

## CONCRETE PATIOS AND WALKS

Concrete patios and walks should be inspected regularly for dusting, spalling, cracking, and settling. Patios and walks constructed of concrete require comparatively little maintenance if the concrete mix had the proper composition and was correctly poured and cured. If they are exposed to severe abrasion, heavy vehicle loads, or similar wear conditions, however, they can develop problems.

One of the more common problems with concrete floors is the development of unsightly cracks, which can be caused by shrinkage, temperature changes, settlement, or lack of rigidity. When such movements are recurrent and can be eliminated only by major structural changes, little can be done except to keep the cracks filled with a mastic material. In many cases comparatively small cracks can be filled with varnish or resin. Although the cracks will remain visible, they will not leak or gather dirt. When the cause of larger cracks has been determined and corrective measures have been taken to eliminate further cracking, the cracks can be permanently repaired by filling them with nonshrinking cement mortar.

Patching will not permanently correct cracks in slabs on grade caused by vertical movement resulting from exceeding the design load of the slab, inadequacy of the base, or insufficient bearing capacity of the soil. Slab failure under these circumstances can be corrected only by a major maintenance operation, such as mudjacking.

Surface cracks that are not structural defects must be promptly filled to maintain a watertight surface. Thoroughly clean the crack with a high-pressure water jet to remove all foreign matter. Edges of the crack should be moistened but not wet. Fill the crack with a thin grout of cement and water, using a brush if necessary to push the grout into the crack. For wider cracks, use a mortar of cement, sand, and water instead of cement grout. If cracks

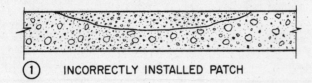

① INCORRECTLY INSTALLED PATCH

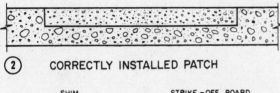

② CORRECTLY INSTALLED PATCH

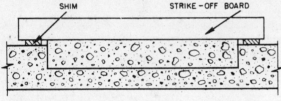

③ CORRECT METHOD OF SCREEDING PATCH

*Correct and incorrect methods of patching concrete are shown above.*

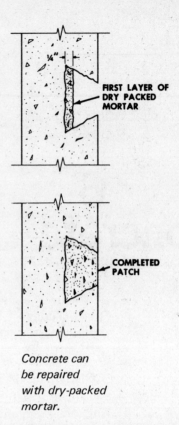

*Concrete can be repaired with dry-packed mortar.*

are not wide enough to permit placement of filler material, they should be cut out prior to cleaning. After filling the crack, cover it with burlap or sand, and keep the covering moist for at least three days.

## CONCRETE WALLS

Normally, concrete walls require a minimum amount of maintenance. Cut out cracks to a depth of 1 inch and a width of at least $1/2$ inch. Wet down before filling with a sand-cement mortar (two parts sand, one part cement). Repair large broken areas by cutting out sufficiently to expose reinforcing rods or mesh that will bind the new concrete to the remaining wall. Thoroughly clean and wet the cut surfaces of the wall, then coat with a slurry of neat cement and water prior to placing the new material. Most defects that cause appreciable problems, such as leakage, are due to the expansion and contraction of the building members with temperature changes.

### Efflorescence

Efflorescence on walls always indicates trouble. It usually appears as a light powder or crystallization after the evaporation of water.

Excess moisture in the walls may come from defective flashings, gutters, downspouts, copings, or improperly filled joints.

Locating the source of the moisture can require a bit of work. The water may not be entering the wall at the point where the efflorescence occurs. Streaks on the wall from the top down or wet patches some distance from the top may indicate defective gutters or copings. Patches of efflorescence are sometimes caused by opened joints. Water may also enter through windowsills or around window and door frames. Efflorescence close to the ground may indicate ground water drawn up by capillary action.

Concrete walls that have an "open" texture may be made more durable, more attractive, and more watertight by painting with portland cement paint.

### Cracks

Lack of adequate expansion and contraction joints is a common cause of cracking. Other common causes are settlement, poor materials, structural weaknesses in the foundation, excessive floor loads, and poor workmanship in the original construction.

Horizontal movement cracks are usually long, wide cracks that occur along the line of the floor or roof slab, or along the line of lintels over windows. Vertical and diagonal movement cracks generally occur near the ends or offsets of buildings. They may also be found extending from a windowsill to the lintel of a door or window on a lower floor. These vary from $1/8$ to $3/8$ inches in width. Do not use brittle materials to repair such cracks; use a flexible compound.

Shrinkage cracks are fine, hairline cracks. In repairing shrinkage cracks, do not chisel them out and fill them. Instead, scrub with a grout made with 65 percent cement and 35 percent sand mixed to a consistency of heavy molasses. Wet the wall and scrub in the mixture, then cure it with water. Postpone shrinkage crack repairs until the wall is at least one year old to avoid repeating the repair job. In special cases, such as when the concrete is exposed to severe weathering or corrosion, you should repair broken or spalled concrete as soon as practicable to prevent progressive deterioration that might result from the rusting of the reinforcing steel. Seal cracks to water that would promote corrosion and subject the concrete to the danger of further deterioration by freezing and thawing.

### Spalled and Eroded Surfaces

Treat spalled and eroded surfaces that cannot be renewed by brush coats of thick cement water paint by plastering them with a mix of one part portland cement, two to two and a half parts of masonry sand, and 10 percent hydrated lime. Apply the plaster in layers $3/8$ to $3/4$ inch thick and then cure it.

Prior to beginning the plaster work, (1) remove all loose and fractured surface material with a hand chisel or air hammer, (2) clean and repair all exposed steel, and (3) roughen the remaining smooth surfaces with a wire brush or by sandblasting. Patch all deep recesses. After the patches have attained an initial set, saturate the defective surface with water for an hour or two before plastering.

## MIXES

The characteristics of concrete should be considered on a relative basis as well as in terms of the quality required for a particular construction or repair project. A single batch of concrete does not offer maximum strength, durability, and economy. For example, entrained air makes handling easier and is threefore conducive to economy, entrained air promotes watertightness, but entrained air makes concrete less dense and thereby reduces the strength. The goal is to achieve an optimum balance of all the elements.

An example of the simplest form of concrete batching is the mixing of a very small amount of concrete using the 1:2:4 carpenter's mix. The relative volumes of cement, sand, and gravel can be measured in bucketfuls, or even in shovelfuls, and water can be added to give reasonable consistency. A more refined procedure is to fabricate a cubic-foot wooden measuring box to give you greater control over the quantities of the ingredients. To mix approximately one cubic yard of 1:2:4 concrete, you use the "Rule of 42":

| | |
|---|---|
| Cement | 6 bags |
| Sand | 12 cubic feet |
| Gravel | 24 cubic feet |
| | 42 cubic feet of material |

In addition to the carpenter's mix, there are other popular rule-of-thumb mixes:

| | |
|---|---|
| 1:1:2 | a very rich mix; use when great strength is required |
| 1:2:5 | a medium mix; use in large slabs and walls |
| 1:3:5 | a lean mix; use in large foundations or as a backing for masonry |
| 1:4:8 | a very lean mix; use only in mass placings. |

You need certain information before you can proportion a concrete mixture. The size and shape of structural members, the concrete strength required, and the exposure conditions must be determined. This information determines the water-cement ratio, the aggregate characteristics, the amount of entrained air,

## Principal Properties of Various Concrete Mixes

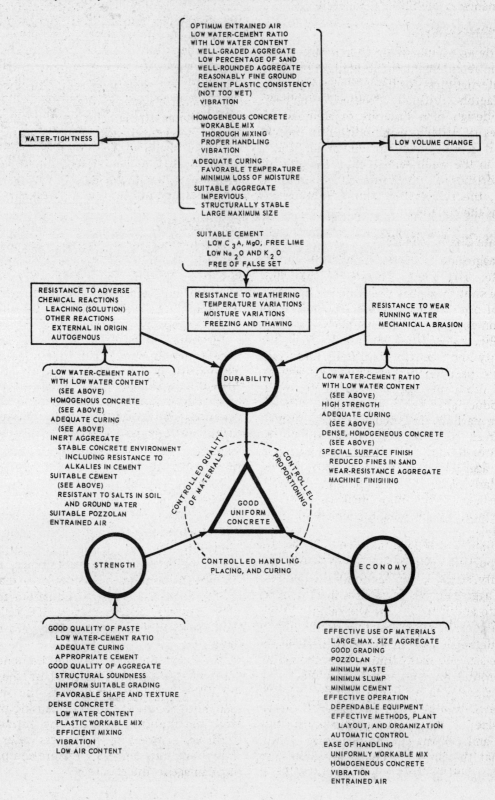

and slump, which are significant factors in the performance of the finished concrete.

## Water-Cement Ratio

In arriving at the water-cement ratio, consider the requirements of strength, durability, and watertightness for the hardened concrete. These factors are usually specified by engineers in the design of a structure or assumed for purposes of arriving at tentative mix proportions. It is important to remember that a change in the water-cement ratio changes the characteristics of the hardened concrete. In general, the rule is that adding more water weakens the concrete.

## Aggregate Characteristics

The aggregate is the sand and stone in the concrete. The shape, surface texture, and soundness of the aggregate influence the properties of both fresh and hardened concrete. In fresh concrete it will influence the workability of the mix. In hardened concrete it affects the durability and strength. Very sharp and rough aggregate particles or flat elongated particles require more fine aggregate to fill the voids and produce a workable mix, than do particles that are partially rounded or cubical. Stones that break up into long slivers should be avoided or should be limited to about 15 percent in aggregate. Flat pieces of aggregate are particularly objectionable in pavement or slabs because heavy loads may break them out of the surface, leaving shallow cavities in the concrete.

The grading and maximum size of aggregate are important because of its effect on the durability, strength, and economy of concrete.

Fine aggregate fills the spaces in the coarse aggregate and increases the workability of the mix. In general, aggregates that do not have a severe deficiency or an excess of particles in any one size and that permit a smooth grading curve produce the most satisfactory mix.

The largest size of coarse aggregate that is practical should be used. The larger the maximum size of the coarse aggregate, the less mortar and cement will be necessary. It follows that the larger the coarse aggregate, the less water and cement will be required for a given quality of concrete. The largest aggregate particle should not exceed one-fifth of the minimum dimension of the member, or three-fourths of the clear space between reinforcing bars. For pavement or floor slabs, the largest aggregate particle should not exceed one-third the slab thickness. The maximum size of coarse aggregate that produces concrete of maximum strength for a given cement content depends upon aggregate source as well as aggregate shape and grading. For many aggregates, this best maximum size is about $3/4$ inch. However, a maximum size of $1^1/_2$ inch aggregate is satisfactory for use in pavements.

## Entrained Air

Entrained air, or air bubbles incorporated in the mix, should be present in all concrete exposed to freezing and thawing and may be used for mild exposure conditions to improve workability. It is recommended for all paving concrete regarding of climatic conditions.

Air-entrained concrete is a comparatively recent development used to reduce scaling, particularly in areas where concrete must survive severe frost action and the harmful effects of chemicals used for melting snow and ice. Air-entrained concrete is more durable but slightly weaker than normal portland cement concrete. The air-entrained mix has better workability and less segregation, but control in handling it is more critical.

Air-entrained concrete consists of cement, fine aggregate, coarse aggregate, and an admixture such as neutralized vinsoll resin (NVR solution). The addition of such mixtures produces millions of tiny air bubbles, ranging from a few microns to 75 microns in diameter, in the cement mixture. Calculations indicate that there are approximately 600 billion air bubbles incorporated in a cubic yard of concrete.

The freeze-thaw resistance of hardened concrete is significantly improved by the use of intentionally entrained air. As the water in concrete freezes, it expands, causing pressure that can rupture concrete. The entrained-air voids act as reservoirs for excess water forced into them, thus relieving pressure and preventing damage to the concrete.

When mixing water is held constant, the entrainment of air will increase slump. When cement content and slump are held constant, less mixing water is required; the resulting decrease in the water-cement ratio helps to offset possible strength decreases and results in improvements in other paste properties such as permeability. Hence, the strength of air-entrained concrete may equal, or nearly equal, that of regular concrete when their cement content and slump is the same.

### Slump

The term "slump" refers to a way of measuring the consistency of concrete. A slump test should not be used to compare mixes of wholly different proportions or mixes with different kinds and sizes of aggregates. When used to evaluate different batches of the same mixture, changes in slump indicate changes in materials, mix proportions, or water content.

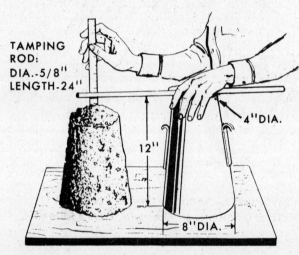

TAMPING ROD: DIA.-5/8" LENGTH-24"

4"DIA.

12"

8"DIA.

*Slump test to measure consistency of concrete*

### CURING

Curing fresh concrete helps to protect it from surface checking and cracking, excessive water loss, and damage by heavy rains, flowing water, and temperature extremes. The most favorable temperature for curing concrete is 70° to 80° F.

Cure concrete made with standard portland cement for at least five days. Concrete made

with high-early-strength cement should be cured for a minimum of three days. In extremely high or low temperatures, it may be necessary to cure for twice as long as the above recommendations. Depending on the availability of materials and local conditions, protect and cure concrete as soon as it has set. Use one or more of the following methods of curing.

### Water Curing

Keep the concrete continuously wet with water-saturated material or keep it wet with mechanical sprinklers, by flooding, or by some other means. Do not use a method of periodic wetting. Use clean water that is free of any substances that might cause staining or discoloration.

### Saturated-Sand Curing

Cover the concrete surface with at least an inch of sand. Keep the sand spread evenly and continuously saturated during the curing period.

### Fabric Curing

Cotton quilts for curing concrete are made of two sheets of heavy, coarse-woven fabric stitched over a layer of low-grade cotton batting. Lay the cotton quilts with lapped joints and keep them wet.

### Paper Curing

Two-ply kraft paper for curing concrete is usually reinforced between plies with fiber strands in two directions and sealed with asphalt. Lay kraft sheets with 4-inch laps. Cement the joints with waterproof glue or hold them together with heavy gummed paper strips.

### Curing Compounds

Do not use curing compounds on surfaces to which additional concrete is to be bonded or on vertical surfaces exposed to sunshine and wind.

### FORMWORK

Formwork is a temporary structure that supports its own weight and that of the freshly

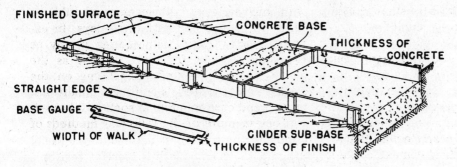

FINISHED SURFACE    CONCRETE BASE
                                THICKNESS OF
                                  CONCRETE
STRAIGHT EDGE
BASE GAUGE
WIDTH OF WALK
                        CINDER SUB-BASE
            THICKNESS OF FINISH

*Forms for pouring a concrete sidewalk*

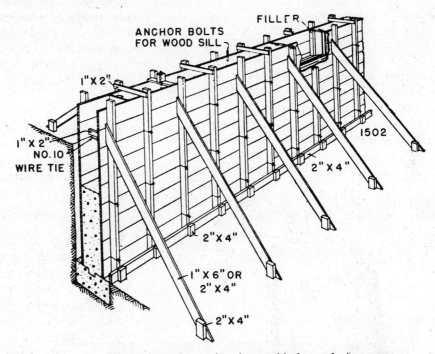

ANCHOR BOLTS          FILLER
FOR WOOD SILL

1" X 2"

1" X 2"
NO. 10
WIRE TIE

1502

2" X 4"

2" X 4"

1" X 6" OR
2" X 4"

2" X 4"

*The earth can be used as the outside form of a basement
or cellar wall if it is firm enough. Otherwise, build a formwork.*

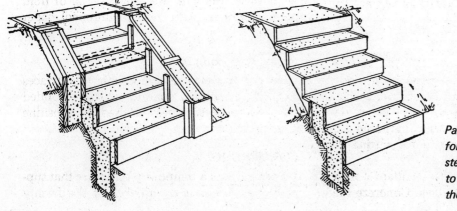

*Parts of these forms
for earth-supported
steps are cut away
to show
the construction.*

placed concrete as well as the live loads imposed upon it by materials, equipment, and workmen. Whether or not you need a supporting form depends on the size of the job. If, for example, you are patching small cracks in a wall, a form would not be necessary. On the other hand, if you are replacing steps, formwork will be necessary. In general, formwork is needed for any extensive vertical concrete work.

Practically all formwork jobs require lumber. Any lumber that is straight, structurally strong, and sound can be used for formwork. Lumber that comes in contact with the concrete should be surfaced on at least one side and on both edges. The surfaced side is turned toward the concrete. All wood forms that have not been treated should be wet before the concrete is poured.

The time required for concrete members to reach safe strengths varies with the type of cement used, the concrete mixture, the atmospheric temperature during pouring and curing, and the type of structure. Forms usually should remain in place longer for reinforced concrete than for plain mass concrete. Horizontal work needs more time than does vertical work to cure and to attain the proper strength to support its own weight plus imposed loads.

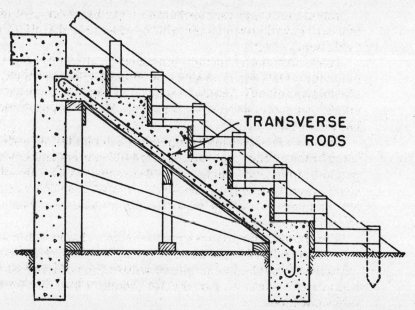

TRANSVERSE RODS

Forms for self-supporting steps

# 7
# Termites

Ground-nesting, or subterranean, termites occur throughout the United States. They flourish in the South Atlantic and Gulf Coast states and in California.

Their chief food is cellulose obtained from wood, as in the woodwork of buildings. One way to thwart the immense damage they do is to construct buildings properly. Another way is to treat the soil near foundations and under concrete slabs with chemicals. Action against termites begins with knowing what they are.

Termites are social insects that live in colonies or nests in the soil, from which they obtain moisture. The adult workers and soldiers are wingless, grayish white, and similar to ants in appearance. The soldiers have much larger heads and longer mandibles, or jaws, than the workers. The workers are the ones that destroy wood and are usually seen when a piece of infested wood is examined.

The reproductives, or sexual adults, have yellowish brown to black bodies and two pairs of long, whitish, opaque wings of equal size. They often are mistaken for ants, but the reproductive forms of true ants have two pairs of transparent wings of unequal size. Termites have thick waistlines. Ants have thin waistlines.

The first signs of an infestation may be the swarming of large numbers of winged reproductives from a building, the appearance of discarded wings on the floor beneath doors and windows, or the presence of flattened, earthen shelter tubes over the surface of foundations.

Often you cannot see termite damage on the surface of wood. You have to look inside. The workers build galleries within the materials they attack. Occasionally they honeycomb timbers completely and leave little more than a thin shell. Grayish specks of excrement and earth cover the insides of the galleries. Subterranean termites do not reduce the wood to a powdery mass or push wood particles to the outside, as do some other wood-boring insects.

Termites enter buildings through flat, earthen shelter tubes that the workers construct over the surfaces of foundations, through cracks and joints and aruond plumbing in concrete slabs, and through wood that connects the soil with the woodwork of the building.

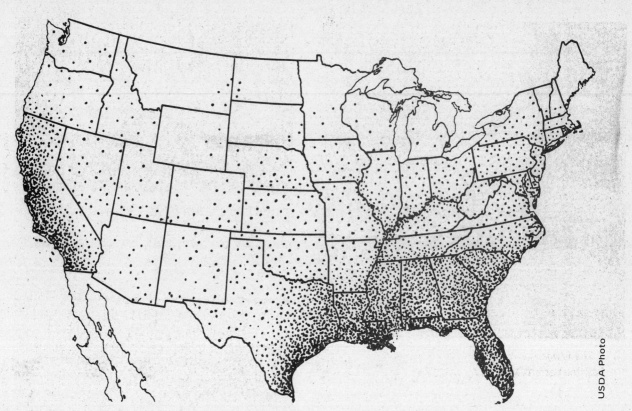

*The hazard of ground-nesting termite infestation in the United States is most prominent in the South Atlantic and Gulf Coast states and in California.*

## PREVENTIVE MEASURES

Remove all tree roots, stumps, and other wood debris from the building site before construction starts. Remove grade stakes, frame boards, and scraps of lumber. If no wood is left in or on the soil, the danger of an infestation is reduced.

Prevent moisture from accumulating in the soil under a building. Slope the soil surface so that moisture will drain away from the building.

Choose foundations carefully. Poured, properly reinforced concrete foundations are best. If hollow blocks, brick foundations, or piers are used, cap them with at least 4 inches of reinforced poured concrete, or fill the top course of blocks and all joints completely with concrete to prevent attack through poor mortar and through hollows in blocks.

The beams and girders of buildings with crawl space under them should be at least 12 inches above the ground. The bottoms of floor joists should be at least 18 inches above the ground. Make the outside gradeline at least 6 inches below all exterior woodwork.

In places where the termite hazard is extreme, the use of pressure-treated sills, joists, and headers is an additional safeguard.

Provide good ventilation underneath buildings with crawl space. In general, the net area of ventilation openings should be $1/160$ of the ground area beneath the building. Distribute the vents so that no dead-air pockets are formed.

Concrete slab-on-ground construction is susceptible to termite attack, and infestations are difficult to control. Slabs vary in susceptibility to penetration by termites. The monolithic type is best, because the floor and the footings are poured in one operation, and there are no joints to permit entry. The suspended slab is fair. The floor and the foundation are poured

The adult soldier guards the colony.

*The winged sexual, or reproductive, adult of the eastern subterranean termite*

The adult worker is usually found when the infested wood is examined.

This piece of wood reveals extensive tunneling by termites along the grain.

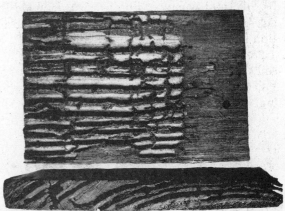

Inside the damaged wood, specks of excrement are found on the walls of the galleries.

*Termites are entering the void in the wall around the pipe.*

*When this shelter tube was removed, termites were exposed.*

separately, but the floor extends across the top of the foundation. This prevents hidden termite entry. The floating slab is the most hazardous. It may rest on a ledge of the foundation or be independent of it. Termites can enter at the joint between the slab and the foundation.

Because settlement cracks almost always occur in any type of slab and termites can enter through them, you should treat the soil with chemicals before pouring the concrete of any slab.

Water emulsions of any of these formulations will give many years of protection: aldrin, 0.5 percent; chlordane, 1 percent; dieldrin, 0.5 percent; and heptachlor, 0.5 percent. These chemicals are sold as concentrated solutions, which can be diluted with water to the desired concentrations.

Apply 4 gallons of the water emulsion per 10 linear feet to the soil along the inside and outside of the perimeter foundation, along the interior foundation, and around the places where plumbing comes through the slab. Apply 1 gallon per 10 square feet as an overall treatment.

## REMEDIAL MEASURES

If your house is infested with termites, there are a number of steps you can take to control the problem. Remove all scraps of wood, formboards, and other debris containing cellulose under and near the building. Remove any wooden units, such as rtellises, that connect the ground to the woodwork of the building, and replace them to break those contacts. Replace structurally weakened sills, joists, flooring, and other members with sound materials. Fill voids, cracks, or expansion joints in concrete or masonry with cement or roofing-grade coal tar pitch. Provide drainage and ventilation.

The chemicals used to prevent attack can be used also to control existing infestations. Buildings with crawl spaces very often can be treated easily and effectively.

1. Dig trenches 6 to 8 inches wide around all piers and pipes and along both the inside and the outside of all foundation walls. For poured concrete foundations, the trench need be only 3 to 4 inches deep. For foundations of brick and of hollow block masonry, it should be at least 12 inches deep. Where the footing is more than 12 inches deep, use a crowbar, pipe, or rod to make holes about a foot apart and extend them from the bottom of the trench to the footing. This will prevent termites from gaining hidden entry to the building through voids in these types of foundations. Never dig the trench below the top of the footing.
2. Pour one of the chemicals into the trench at the rate of 4 gallons per 10 linear feet for each foot of depth. If the trench is deep, apply the chemical to alternate layers of about 6 inches of soil.
3. To treat basements, dig a trench 6 to 8 inches wide and about a foot deep along the outside wall and close to it. Then with a crowbar, pipe, or rod, make holes about a foot apart from the bottom of the trench to the footing. Pour the chemical into the trench at the rate of 4 gallons per 10 linear feet for each foot of depth from grade to footing; alternately replace and treat 6-inch layers of soil.

Infestations in houses built with a slab on the ground are hard to control, because it is not easy to place chemicals in the soil under such floors where they will be effective.

One way to do it is to drill holes about $1/2$ inch in diameter through the concrete slab close to the points where the termites are or where they may be entering. Space the holes about 6 inches away from the wall and about 12 inches apart to ensure proper treatment of the soil underneath. Take care to avoid drilling into plumbing and electric conduits. Apply the chemical through the holes by any practical means available.

Another way is to drill through the outside foundation walls to the soil just under the slab and pour the chemical into the holes.

These methods are complicated and usually require special equipment. You may need to employ the services of a well-established, reliable pest control operator for such jobs.

Infestations often occur at porches, terraces, and entrance platforms. The best way to control infestations there is to tunnel under the concrete slab next to the foundation wall, all the way from one side to the other, and apply a chemical in the bottom of the tunnel or trench. Remove all wood debris you encounter in digging the tunnel. Place an access panel over the opening to permit annual inspections and additional soil treatments, if needed.

Another way is to drill holes 12 inches apart, either through the adjacent foundation wall from within the crawl space or basement or through the entrance slab, and introduce the chemical through the holes.

## DRYWOOD TERMITES AND POWDER-POST BEETLES

Drywood termites and powder-post beetles also attack the woodwork of buildings. Their damage may be mistaken for that caused by subterranean termites. Drywood termites occur most abundantly in southern Florida and along the coast of California. They do not require contact with the soil as do the subterranean forms.

Their damage can be recognized by clean cavities cut across the grain in comparatively solid wood and the presence of slightly compressed pellets in the cavities. Some of the pellets are pushed outside through small openings and often form piles on surfaces below.

Localized infestations can be controlled by injecting 5 percent DDT, 2 percent chlordane, or 5 percent pentachlorophenol in No. 2 fuel oil into the cavities or by thoroughly brushing the surface with one or more applications.

Powder-post beetles occur throughout the United States. They attack both softwoods and hardwoods. The adult insects are seldom seen. The whitish larvae, or grubs, work within the wood and reduce it to fine or to coarse powder, which is packed in the galleries or pushed to the exterior through small holes. The presence of this dust on the surface usually is the first sign of an infestation.

You can control local infestation by brushing or spraying the infested places thoroughly

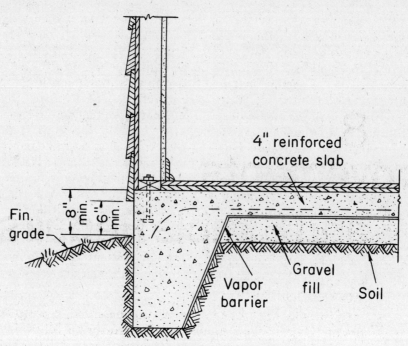

4" reinforced
concrete slab

Fin.
grade

8" min.

6" min.

Vapor
barrier

Gravel
fill

Soil

*For slab-on-ground construction,
the monolithic type is best, because
there are no joints that would allow
termites to enter.*

with 5 percent DDT, 2 percent chlordane, or 0.5 percent dieldrin in No. 2 fuel oil or deodorized kerosene. More than one application may be necessary if the infestation is deepseated.

If infestations of drywood termites or powder-post beetles are spread throughout a building, fumigation is the most practical method of control. The service of a licensed pest control operator is required for fumigation.

All of the chemicals that have been mentioned are poisonous to people and animals. Handle them carefully. If the chemicals accidentally come in contact with skin or eyes, wash the skin immediately with warm, soapy water and the eyes with plenty of water or with a solution containing a teaspoonful of boric acid per glassful of warm water.

# 8
# Improvements
# and Simple Repairs

## WOOD DOORS

Exterior doors are more subject to abuse and to weathering than interior doors. Exterior doors should be inspected for the following defects: poor fitting, including deteriorated or damaged frames; paint deterioration; material damage, such as cracked or broken glass, split or cracked wood panels, warped or dented metal, and warped or broken screening; and broken or inoperative hardware, such as locks, hinges, and slides. In addition, check all the doorstops, the thresholds, and the weather stripping for cracks, looseness, and workability.

Mechanical injury to mullions, headers, jambs, or hardware usually causes trouble. Decay, resulting from exposure to weather or from shrinkage of door members, also causes distortion or failure. Frequently, the free edge of the door sags and causes the door to bind at the bottom and to open at the top. When you are inspecting such doors, the following checks should be made:

1. Examine the jamb opening to see that the hinge and lock sides are plumb and parallel.
2. Check the door header to see that it is level.
3. Check anchorage of the jamb and the hinges.
4. Check lock faceplates for projection beyond the face of the door.
5. Check all members for swelling, shrinking, or warping.

Settling of the foundation or shrinkage and deflection of framing members often causes trouble at door openings. When the greatest settlement is on the hinge side of a door, the door will tend to become floor-bound at the lock side. When settlement is greatest on the lock side, the door will bind at the head jamb. As a result, the bolt in the lock will not be in alignment with the strike plate, making it impossible to lock the door securely. Vertical settlement and horizontal deflection will cause the jamb opening to become out of square. On most wood doors the simple correction is to plane as required at either the top or bottom for proper clearance.

### Warping

The following procedures apply when the door itself has shrunk or is warped or swollen, or has sagged.

1. When a door shrinks, remove the hinge leaves and install a filler (cardboard or metal shim) at the outer edge of the jamb and hinge mortise. This forces the door closer to the jamb at the lock edge and, provided hinge pins do not bind, the door should then operate satisfactorily. Each hinge should be shimmed equally to prevent the door from becoming hinge-bound. When the door has swelled, place shims in the inner edge of the hinge mortise.

2. Restore a warped door to its normal shape by removing the door and laying it flat. Weighting the door down may also be necessary. If the door is still warped after a reasonable length of time, battens screwed to the door will help restore it to true plane. Screw eyes, rods, and turnbuckles will also help straighten a door by gradually pulling it into place.

3. Install a diagonal batten brace from the top of the lock side to the bottom of the hinge side to repair a sagging door permanently. The diagonal brace must cover the joint between the rail and the stile and it must be securely fastened to both members, at the top and the bottom, and to the other intermediate rail members. Temporary repair is made by the installation of a wire stay brace equipped with turnbuckles that is placed diagonally in the reverse direction from a batten brace.

4. The doors or door members may require rebuilding because of neglect or abuse. Remove the door to a flat surface and then replace the damaged member. Carpenter's clamps will assist in holding the door members square while the nails or screws are driven.

5. Trim the door when the preceding methods fail to correct the trouble. However, do not cut doors immediately following rain or in damp weather. When dry, the door may fit too loosely.

### WOOD DECKS AND FLOORING

Wood floors should be checked for loose nails; warped, cupped, or loose boards; raised ends; slivers, cracks, loose knots, or raised nails; and water or other damage from improper cleaning, condensation, and wood decay. If floor damage requires replacement of strips or planks, the following procedures should be observed:

1. Make two longitudinal cuts in the damaged strip or plank.

2. Remove the section between the two cuts by cutting the strip with a chisel at midpoint.

3. Remove the remainder of the damaged strip, taking care not to damage the tongues and grooves of adjoining boards.

4. Remove the lower part of the groove of the new closure strip or plank.

5. Insert the tongue of the closure into the groove of the adjoining board and nail with two 8-penny annular ring finishing nails through the top surface. When possible, the end joints should be located so that the nails will enter the joint. In new closure areas of flooring laid in mastic on concrete, remove the existing mastic and apply new mastic of the type recommended by the flooring manufacturer before installing the new closure.

6. Set exposed nails.

7. Dress the new portion to the level of the adjacent floor by sanding both areas to a continuous, smooth plane.

8. Dry-sweep the area to remove all particles of dust.

9. On open-grained woods, brush on a paste filler. After the filler has partially dried, rub it into the pores of the wood with a circular motion. Wipe the surface lightly to remove any surplus filler. Inadequate filling is indicated by pockmarks and results from wiping off too much of the filler or from unusual absorption by the wood. Eliminate such deficiencies by repeating the filler application.

10. Seal the floor with a wax, stain, or other material.

## WINDOWS

Windows should be inspected for loose-fitting or damaged frames; ill-fitting or broken sash; cracked or broken glass; deteriorated putty or caulking; broken or worn sash balances; and missing or broken hardware.

Window failures may result from various causes. The most common cause is weathering, which causes loss of putty, paint, and caulking. This leads to subsequent deterioration and rotting in wood windows and rusting in metal windows. If atmospheric conditions cause ordinary putty to deteriorate quickly, plastic glazing compound should be substituted. Caulking around window frames must be maintained in good order to prevent leakage of moisture and air. Rust spots on metal sash and frames should be wire-brushed or sanded, cleaned with a rag saturated with mineral spirits, and then painted. Problems of alignment caused by building settlement must be adjusted in conjunction with overall corrective measures, which may involve stabilizing the foundation and framing.

## BASEMENT DOORS

Basement doors are important because they provide direct, easy access to storage and living areas. However, they can develop problems that necessitate repairs or replacement. One good solution to problem basement doors is to replace them with Bilco doors. It is comparatively simple to install a modern Bilco basement door.

If you are replacing an existing basement entrance, examine the condition of the concrete areaway under your present hatchway. If this areaway is uneven or crumbling, it should be recapped with fresh concrete to assure a

*Black & Decker*

*Caulk around window frames to prevent damage caused by water or air.*

*When replacing an old window, fill voids with trimmers spaced to accommodate the width of the new window.*

*Andersen Corporation, Bayport, Minnesota*

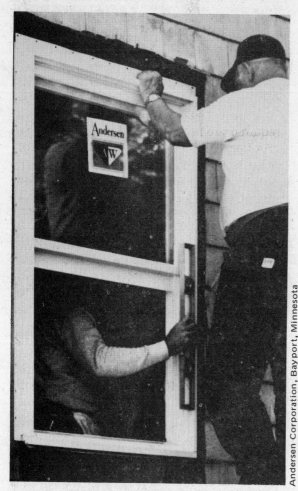

*Set the window into the opening and nail
at one of the corners; then, square
and plumb the window with a level
while the final adjustment is made.*

*Break away short pieces of wall shingles
at the sides of the new window so that new,
wider shingles can be inserted to fill
the gap around the window frame.*

leakproof seal. You can use premixed concrete for this purpose. Then follow these steps:

1. Remove the old door and, if necessary, the top of the areaway. A crowbar may be needed to accomplish this.
2. Assemble the Bilco door frame, using the materials that are included in the package.
3. Put the assembled door frame in its proper position over the areaway. Cut the siding so that the header flange will fit up between the sheathing and the siding. If the exterior wall is masonry, the header must be caulked or flashed.

4. Build a simple wood frame around the top of the areaway and put the frame back in place, blocking it up to correct height. Bricks are ideal for this because they will reduce the amount of concrete required. Pour new capping and imbed screws with spring nuts in the wet concrete.
5. Attach the doors to the frame and check that bottom edges of both doors form a straight line. If not, move the front of the unit slightly left or right for the proper alignment.
6. When the concrete has set, engage the torsion bars in the clips on the side pieces,

according to the instructions. The torsion bars make the doors extremely easy to open and close.

7. Remove the form boards. Caulk around the outside of the door where it joins the masonry and the house wall. Then finish in the desired color with an alkyd-base metal enamel.

If your present areaway is level and flat, and the concrete is in good repair, it will not be necessary to recap. Mix a small batch of concrete with a bonding agent and patch any holes in the existing concrete. Then follow these steps:

1. Assemble the Bilco door and place it on the areaway. Mark and cut out the siding so that the door header will be between the siding and the sheathing. If the exterior wall is masonry, the header must be caulked or flashed.
2. Slide the Bilco door in place with the header between the siding and the sheathing. Attach the doors to the frame and move the front of the unit left or right if necessary, so that the bottom edges of both doors form a straight line. Mark hole locations in the side flanges and the sill.
3. Mark and drill holes in the side pieces and the sill. Slide the assembled frame off the areaway.
4. Drill holes with a star drill. You can drill the holes with the unit in place if you use a pistol drill with a $1/4$-inch carbide-tip masonry bit. Insert plastic shields in the holes. Replace the unit on areaway and secure it with screws. Caulk and apply alkyd enamel.

Most homeowners who have experienced the benefits of an outside basement entrance will be interested in adding it to any home that does not have this feature. It is especially important if a workshop or recreation room is planned, or if a swimming pool figures in the family's future. Equipment and furnishings go in and out directly, with no traffic through first floor rooms. A route to safety is provided in the event of an emergency. To create a basement entrance where one does not exist, the following procedures should be used:

1. Select the proper size Bilco door and stair stringers for the grade height and basement depth. Excavate to dimensions about one foot greater than the outside dimensions of required areaway, to leave room for waterproofing the walls. Use concrete blocks for the new areaway.
2. Cut the opening in the foundation to the proper width for the door size. Remove this section of wall with a sledgehammer, preferably from inside the basement.
3. Build a 12-inch wide concrete footing to provide a firm level base for the first course of concrete blocks. Place a drainage system around the footing as provided on the original foundation. Proceed to build the block walls.
4. Install the Bilco door in accordance with the installation instructions in the door package by pouring the concrete capping on the wall, or capping it with solid 4-inch concrete block. Install the Bilco stair stringers as instructed in the stringer package. Then, install a plywood door at the base of the steps. This functions in conjunction with the Bilco door to prevent heat loss.

## CHIMNEYS

Chimneys should be inspected every fall for defects. Check for loose or fallen bricks, cracked or broken flue lining, and excessive soot accumulation by lowering an electric light into the flue. Mortar joints can be tested from the outside by prodding with a knife.

If inspection shows defects that cannot be readily repaired or reached for repair, you should tear the masonry down and rebuild it properly. Do not use the old bricks that have been impregnated with soot and creosote in the new work, because these bricks will stain the plaster whenever dampness occurs. You will find it is almost impossible to remove soot and creosote stains.

Chimney cleaning usually is not necessary in the average home. But should it become necessary, vacuuming by a commercial cleaning firm is the best and cleanest method.

*Use a crowbar to remove old basement door.*

*With frame in place mark position of screws. Remove frame; drill holes; replace frame; secure with screws.*

*After frame is in place and secure, attach doors.*

*After door is completely installed, it can be painted with an alkyd-base metal enamel.*

Stair stringers may be installed
after Bilco door is in place
to make access to basements and
family rooms easier.

If there is not too great an offset in the chimney, you can dislodge soot and loose material by pulling a weighted sack of straw up and down in the flue. Seal the front of a fireplace when cleaning the flue to keep soot out of the room.

Chemical soot removers are not particularly recommended. They are not very effective in removing soot from chimneys and they cause soot to burn, which creates a fire hazard. Some, if applied to soot at high temperatures and in sufficient quantity, may produce uncontrollable combustion and even an explosion. Common rock salt is not the most effective remover, but it is widely used, because it is cheap, readily available, and easy to handle. Use 2 or 3 teacupsful per application.

Creosote may form in chimneys, especially when wood is burned and in cold weather. It is very hard to remove. The only safe method is to chip it from the masonry with a blade, and you must be careful not to knock out mortar joints or damage the flue lining.

# 9
# Foundations and Basements

A foundation supports the weight of the house and other vertical loads, such as snow. It stabilizes the house against horizontal forces, such as wind. It is a retaining wall that supports the earth fill around the house. It is often a cellar wall that bars moisture, heat loss, or sound transmission.

## TYPES

The most common foundation is the continuous wall which may be built of stone, clay tile, block, brick, or concrete. Recently, treated wood, metal, and other materials have been used. Continuous walls are used to support heavy loads or to enclose a crawl space or basement. If enclosure of space is the main objective, then the wall may be built of lighter, more porous insulating materials which will reduce heat loss and sound transmission.

A step foundation is a continuous wall of variable height. It is used on steep grades or for houses with partial basements.

The pier foundation is a series of piers that support the house. They are generally masonry but sometimes they are made of other materials. The pole or post foundation is a special kind of pier foundation built of pressure-treated wood. It is often used on steep terrain where there is considerable variation in the height of the piers and where a regular masonry pier might bend and break.

Beams placed between the piers of a pier foundation support the house. The size of such a beam depends on the load it must carry and the distance between piers. The space between piers is generally enclosed with curtain walls that carry no load and whose main purpose is to enclose the space and act as a barrier to wind, heat, moisture, and sometimes animals.

A grade beam foundation is a pressure-treated wood or reinforced concrete beam that is submerged to a depth of about 8 inches below grade. It may be supported on a stone fill or on underground piers that extend into the ground below the frost line. The grade beam is especially useful in dry climates or well-drained soils where the house can be built close to the ground.

The slab foundation is a special foundation which floats on top of the soil and also serves as the floor of the house. The slab is thickened under all of the walls to support their heavy loads.

A continuous-wall foundation made of wood

*Frost heaving combined with a shallow footing caused this building wall to crack at its weakest point.*

All slab floors are not slab foundations; many are simply concrete floors. A separate foundation supports the wall loads.

Every foundation must support the weight of the house and its contents. This load can vary considerably depending on the type of construction, the kind of furniture, and the special uses to which the house is subjected. In colder climates, the foundation must carry ice and snow that accumulate on the roof. If foundation loads are heavy, reinforced concrete provides the strongest wall. Wider masonry walls carry heavier loads than narrow ones.

Some houses are so heavy that the foundation must be widened at the bottom to keep them from sinking into the soil. The widened bottom of the foundation is called a footing. Its size depends on the kind of soil under it. Soil strengths vary from 1,000 to 12,000 pounds per square foot. In general, footings are designed for 1,000 pounds per square foot, but if you know your soil type, you may design smaller footings.

Thickness of the footing depends on how far it protrudes beyond the foundation wall. The rule is that the thickness should be $1\frac{1}{2}$ times the largest projection.

Since wind may lift or slide a building off its foundation, a house must be securely fastened to its foundation. For masonry walls the fastening devices should be extended through the foundation to the footing. In all cases there should be a continuous tie extending as far into the soil as is practical.

Foundations acting as retaining walls must be designed to prevent overturning or breakage. Breakage may be prevented by reinforcing or by making the wall thicker. Overturning may be prevented by making the wall thicker, tying the wall to anchors in the soil, or counterbalancing the wall.

## REPAIRING AND REMODELING

Foundation repairing or remodeling is frequently a hard job requiring the services of an engineer, builder, or house mover. Often it is necessary to lift the building from the existing foundation and support it by other means until the repair is completed. If an entire foundation is replaced, the new foundation must be expertly constructed to fit the building; if only part of a foundation is replaced, the new part must not only fit the building but be bonded to the rest of the foundation. Digging a basement under a house usually means that the workmen have to work in cramped, close quarters. If the house has a chimney above the area of the new basement, the chimney will

USDA Photo

The sills of a frame building can be broken
or torn loose from the foundation
if the anchor bolts are too small,
are not embedded in the foundation far enough,
or are spaced too far apart.

USDA Photo

Rotten sills and the lower end of the studs
are being replaced in sections,
making the repair job safer and easier
than replacing the foundation
all in one operation.

need special support to keep it from crashing down to the floor of the new basement.

Some foundation repair jobs are alike; others are one-of-a-kind situations. There are a few general pointers, however, that will make many of the jobs safer and easier undertakings.

## Raising and Supporting Buildings

Before you raise a building, unload it. Remove heavy contents and property that is easily damaged.

Next, disconnect electric and telephone wires, plumbing, and masonry steps and porches. Remove the nuts from the bolts that anchor the sills to the foundation.

Make holes through the foundation walls near the original building piers. Slip temporary sills (8- by 8-inch or 12- by 12-inch timbers) through the holes. The temporary sills must extend beyond the walls of the building far enough to be supported on cribbing.

Jack up the temporary sills. This will transfer the weight of the building from the foundation to the timbers.

Support the temporary sills on cribbing (or blocking) built out of 6 by 6s or 4 by 4s. Remove the jacks. Build the cribbing carefully so that it will not rock or tip. Set it on firm, dry ground; 2- by 10-inch planks laid close together on the ground will serve as a footing and distribute the load of the cribbing.

When only a small part of the building is raised, post supports (wood 6 by 6s or 4 by 4s or pipes) are often sufficient, and they obstruct work less than temporary sills and cribbing.

If a sufficient number of jacks are not available to raise the whole building at one time, raise one side a little, set cribbing to hold the raised side in place, and progress around the building, raising each side by stages until the whole building is raised high enough to build the new foundation.

## Rebuilding Masonry Foundation Walls

Masonry foundation walls of large buildings are safely and easily rebuilt if alternate sections 4 feet long and 8 feet apart are replaced one at a time.

Remove a 4-foot section of foundation wall and excavate to the bottom of the footing. Use the same construction methods for rebuilding the section that you would use for a new foundation.

The new footing can be stepped if the ground slopes, but each step of the footing must be level. Concrete is the best material for the footing. The foundation wall, however, will be more easily built from unit masonry.

Masonry buildings should be raised only under the supervision of an experienced building or house mover. Large buildings without cross partitions must have stiff diagonal braces

*Set the cribbing so that it will support the screw jack evenly and firmly on a broad base.*

inside to prevent them from collapsing, and long struts (or guy wires) outside to resist the wind.

## Adding a Basement

When you add a basement under an entire house, build it in sections. It is costly and hazardous to excavate a large basement under an existing building all at one time. While it is usually poor economy to add a large basement to an existing house, a small basement (8 to 10 feet wide, with sufficient space for a furnace) can be added without great cost or labor.

The farther the basement is under the house, the greater the amount of work involved, so locate it near one outside foundation wall. If the basement will be used for heating-plant space, locate it so that the chimney will be accessible from the basement.

Support the building girder, or sill, that spans the length of the basement with I-beams or heavy wood beams. These beams replace the piers that supported the building girder before the basement was dug. The ends of the supporting beams must rest in slots in the top of the new basement walls.

A safe distance must be allowed between the basement walls and the foundation walls that are parallel to them. If the basement wall is too close to the foundation wall, pressure exerted on the soil by the foundation wall will be exerted laterally on the basement wall.

The safe distance depends on the type of soil and on the difference in vertical height between the footing of the foundation wall and the footing of the basement wall.

In loose, sandy soil, do not put the new basement wall closer to a parallel foundation wall than $1^1/_2$ feet for each vertical foot distance between the footings of the two walls. For example, if the new footing is 4 feet lower than the old footing, the foundation wall and the basement wall must be 6 feet apart.

The safe distance per vertical foot difference in damp clay is 2 feet; in mixtures of sand, dry clay, gravel, and ordinary soil it is $1^1/_2$ feet; in decomposed rock, cinders, or ashes it is 1 foot. If the soil becomes very wet, greater distances will be necessary and will have to be determined by an engineer.

When the side walls of the basement are built and the building girders are supported on beams, excavate the basement. Remove the earth from the excavation through an opening in the foundation wall. This opening can later become an outside door to the basement.

Build the rear wall of the basement after the excavation is completed. If the foundation of the house is entirely of piers (with or without curtain walls on the perimeter of the house), four basement walls will be needed.

When a chimney is within the area of a new basement, it must be extended to below the basement floor. During the excavation it must be supported on two or three steel beams. Support the ends of the beams on cribbing.

The exact placement of the beams and cribbing will depend on the headroom and work area under the house. Ordinarily, holes are cut in the masonry of the chimney just above the footing and the beams are inserted through the holes and blocked up. The chimney is then extended to a new footing below the basement floor. After the new chimney extension is strong enough to support the weight of the existing chimney, the beams are withdrawn and the holes are filled.

When you extend piers to a lower level, support the building girders on blocking, tear out the old piers, and build new ones. Start with a footing below the basement floor and build up. Pipe or structural steel piers are easier to build than masonry piers.

When you extend a wall or chimney to a lower level with unit masonry, you will probably have to omit the top course of units on the extension because of the unevenness of the bottom of the old footing. You can fill this space with stiff concrete. A boxlike form will keep the concrete in place until it sets.

When pouring concrete extensions, the projection of the footing is chiseled off plumb with the wall in 12- to 18-inch sections, and the concrete is poured through the chiseled-out sections.

## Repairing Defects

Foundations usually settle excessively or unevenly when their footings are not deep enough to withstand frost heaving or erosion, or when the piers and walls have too little bearing area for the type of soil and building load. Settling may also be caused by rotted wood posts and sills or by defective masonry.

*This well-built pier was securely doweled to its footing, but the anchor bolt to hold the sill was omitted.*

*The anchor bolt was supplied for this sill, but the footing was made in a shallow, round hole.*

*The anchor bolt in this pier did not extend into the pier far enough, and, under strain, the bolt broke out of the pier.*

*The concrete for this pier was made with an aggregate that was too large for the size of the pier.*

It is more economical to relieve an overloaded foundation by installing extra piers than it is to increase the width of the existing footings.

If you add piers to your house foundation, make sure the sills and girders of the house actually rest on both the new and old piers. If the new piers settle a little when the building is lowered onto them, shim them with wedges of slate or flat pieces of hard tile. (Occasionally a pier is made about a half inch higher than its final grade to allow for settling.)

Where the soil under the footing is eroded but the foundation wall is not damaged, ram a mixture of damp—not wet—sandy clay and 5 to 8 percent (by volume) portland cement under the footing. This will provide a firm, secure bearing. Then bank soil against the foundation; bank it high enough for protection from frost. Slope the soil to divert surface and roof water, and pave or sod the banked soil to protect it from wind erosion.

Exposed wood usually deteriorates at joints first and causes metal fasteners to loosen. Remove loose spikes and driftbolts. Treat the holes and affected areas with a preservative. Plug the holes with wood dowels or with tar. Replace the spikes or bolts in new locations.

Cut away sections of unsound sills and replace them with plank patches. If the whole timber has been weakened, replace it.

Untreated wood posts rot rapidly at the ground line. Replace them with treated posts or with masonry piers.

## INSULATION AND VENTILATION

Because concrete is a good heat conductor, you must take special care when concrete slabs are installed close to the soil surface. A sheet of rigid insulation may be installed vertically down the inside of the foundation wall or between the floor slab and the foundation wall and then horizontally under the slab.

Moisture in basement air is particularly troublesome in wet climates. Hot and relatively dry air from outside enters the basement, where its temperature is reduced by several degrees. As air cools, it can't hold as much moisture; thus cooling the air causes it to become quite humid. If such humid air comes in contact with an even cooler surface such as the wall or the floor of the basement, some of its moisture will condense on the cold surface.

This "sweating" creates an atmosphere conducive to the growth of mold and/or fungi and can be quite objectionable. This problem generally goes away in the winter months when the outside air is colder than the inside air. However, there are exceptions. One example is moisture being produced in the house by extensive boiling of water or by frequent use of hot showers. Another is moisture from the soil soaking through the basement wall and evaporating into the air.

High humidity can be dealt with. Dehumidifiers will remove several quarts of moisture per day from the air. But for dehumidification to be economical and effective, the atmosphere must be closed. Doors and windows should be kept shut. Any outside air getting into the basement will bring more moisture in and cause the dehumidifier to work harder.

Another way to deal with moisture is to eliminate cold surfaces in the basement or house. This can be done through insulation. Floors may be covered with felt paper and tile, walls may be insulated and finished.

If you insulate the wall or floor, you must provide a vapor barrier to prevent moisture in the air from flowing through the insulation to the cold surfaces where it will condense under the insulation. A plastic film, some paints, and several other materials can be vapor barriers.

One common example of moisture passing through insulation is the condensation of moisture under a carpet on a basement floor. Many people must take basement carpets up during the summer months to avoid such condensation.

In winter, ventilation can remove excess moisture from the basement or crawl space. Ventilation becomes extremely important if moisture is being produced there. But ventilation brings in cold air and exhausts warm air, so excessive ventilation will carry off a good deal of heat. Ventilation should be used when the problem can't be handled by insulation, or when periods of high moisture production

*Areaways permit windows to ventilate the basement when the outside grade is high.*

are of short duration. It is especially effective when the crawl space is not heated.

Heating the crawl space and insulating the foundation wall can eliminate the need for vents, and probably reduce total heat loss from the house. In this way, air from the living area can be used to ventilate the crawl space, and moisture carried out of the soil will humidify the dry air in the living area.

Another problem is moisture that flows out of the soil into the basement in liquid form either through the wall or the floor. The smart builder will give the foundation every possible advantage against ground or surface moisture by:

1. Providing the house with gutters and down-spouts to carry roof moisture away from the foundation wall.
2. Sloping the grade away from the house on all sides.
3. Using swales or open drainage to carry off surface water.
4. Backfilling behind the foundation wall with porous fill and providing drain tile at the base of the footing below the basement floor level to drain moisture away from the house.

Parging (plastering) the outside of the foundation wall with a rich cement paste will prevent moisture that comes in contact with the wall from soaking into or through it. Waterproof paints and coating should also be used over the parging to increase moisture resistance.

## MAINTENANCE

However well a structure is constructed initially, proper maintenance and repairs are necessary from time to time to keep it in first-class condition. An effective maintenance inspection will disclose whether specific types of maintenance or repairs are needed.

The inspection program should include emergency inspections prior to and following unusual and severe storms where high velocity winds, abnormal tides, and heavy wave action are anticipated or experienced; and when heavy snowstorms and extremely low temperatures are anticipated or experienced. In some instances, an inspection will turn up minor defects which can be corrected promptly to prevent major damage requiring extensive repairs.

Foundations should be inspected at least annually and more often where climate, soil conditions, or changes in building occupancy or structural use present special problems. Evidence of incipient foundation failure may be found during routine inspection of other structural components.

### Foundation Displacement

A foundation should be checked regularly for proper elevation and alignment. Complete failure in a foundation is rare; however, some settling or horizontal displacement may occur. Common causes of foundation movement include: inadequate footings, overloading the structure, excessive ground water that reduces the bearing capacity of soil, inadequate soil cover that fails to protect against frost heaving, and adjacent excavations that allow unprotected bearing soil to shift from under foundations to the excavated area.

Severe, localized foundation displacement may show up in cracked walls, damaged framing connections, sloping floors, sticking doors, and even leakage through a displaced roof.

Corrective actions taken to alleviate foundation displacement include the following:

1. Replace immediately any missing or dislodged part of the foundation; repair cracks or open joints in concrete or masonry foundation walls; replace defective wood members.
2. Provide proper drainage away from buildings and structure.
3. Replace unstable fill around the foundation with clean, properly compacted fill.
4. Remove growing roots of trees or shrubs that may dislodge footings or foundations.
5. Increase the bearing area of inadequate footings.
6. Maintain enough soil cover to keep footings below the freezing zone.
7. Prohibit loads exceeding the design loading of buildings and structures; isolate foundations from heavy machine operations by providing independent footings and foundations for heavy machines. Air-conditioning equipment should be provided with cork or rubber isolation mounts to prevent transmission of vibrations to the structural frame of the building.

When excavations are made near the footings of buildings, care must be taken in removing bearing soil under existing structures. To relieve pressure of the footings on the soil, shoring, underpinning, or needling may be required for temporary stabilization. Sheet piling may be driven and supported laterally to contain the bearing stress in the soil under footings.

Where water erosion removes soil from around and under footings, some means of erosion prevention, such as ditching or use of splash blocks, must be used.

Footings that fail because of insufficient bearing area must have their bearing area increased. The amount of movement in the wall dictates the repairs necessary. Minor settlement, especially when uniform, may require no repair. If serious settlement occurs, the wall may have to be jacked back to its original elevation, a new footing provided, and repairs made to the wall.

*A shallow foundation undermined by erosion*

Improved drainage is the basic solution to the most common ground water problems. Moisture in structures caused by a high water table can be drained away from a foundation by the installation of open-joint tile drains surrounded by loose gravel fill. The drains should be laid so that they drain the water away from footings and walls into a sump with a float-controlled electric pump. To be effective, a tile drain should generally be pitched from a high point around the perimeter of the building to a low point below the floor slab where the sump and pump are located. Where roof drainage causes a foundation water problem, gutters and downspouts should be installed, preferably connected to a storm sewer. Gutters that are improperly hung or allowed to become clogged will overflow and lose their effectiveness. Leaks in gutters should be repaired promptly. Splash blocks or tile drain should be installed in the absence of storm sewer connections to prevent pooling of water below downspouts. The drainage of surface water toward a building can be reversed by sloping the ground surface away from the foundation wall. Where that is not practical, ditching or installing tile drains will serve the same purpose. The general grade of crawl spaces should not be lower than the surrounding area, which should be graded to drain away from the building.

## Material Deterioration

Foundations are subject to deterioration, whether from material or construction deficiencies or from environmental conditions. The deterioration of foundation materials must be observed directly unless the effects are severe enough to cause foundation settling.

A shallow foundation protected by a well-sodded earth bank

Excessive moisture from surface or subsurface sources is a major cause of timber deterioration, providing the necessary condition for wood decay and encouraging insect infestation. Improperly seasoned wood is subject to cracking, splitting, and deflection. Concrete and masonry are subject to cracking, spalling, and settling, particularly under adverse ground and climatic conditions. Steel and other ferrous metals are subject to corrosion in the presence of moisture and sometimes by contact with acid-bearing soils. Signs of corrosion are darkening of the metal, rusting, and pitting.

## CRAWL SPACES

Considerable deterioration extending from the foundation to the building superstructure can be caused by neglect of crawl spaces, especially in climates where it is necessary to enclose the space to maintain comfortable floor temperatures. Unventilated crawl spaces contribute materially to rapid absorption of moisture into structural wood and other materials, and the spaces soon become a natural habitat for fungus growth and termites. Sills, joints, and subflooring may be affected by wood decay. Condensation may occur in the studding spaces above the floor level and cause paint failures.

Crawl spaces should be carefully checked periodically. In checking these spaces, ensure that they are clean, clear, and accessible. An accumulation of rubbish in the space may provide a natural harbor for insects and rodents as well as impeding access and possible inter-

fering with drainage. Scrap wood is a clear invitation to termites.

Look for disorganized storing of any material in crawl spaces. Also, check for accumulations of water that may breed mosquitoes, cause fungus growth, and weaken soil bearing under footings.

Ensure that all ventilation openings are covered with suitable hardware cloth or copper screening to prevent entry of birds and rodents. In addition, see that access doors to crawl spaces are provided with a suitable padlock and kept closed.

In crawl spaces or "dead" areas under basementless structures, moisture control problems other than building drainage develop from condensation of moisture rising from damp soil. The ideal method of preventing ground moisture from entering the building is to provide an impermeable vapor barrier on the warm side of insulation in floors and walls. In existing buildings this is not practical unless it is done in the course of major renovation.

The most practical solution is to provide a soil cover of water-resistant material. Fifty-five pound roll roofing has been the most widely used and successful soil cover; however, recent tests indicate that 0.006-inch polyethylene plastic sheeting is effective and lighter to handle than roofing paper. The effective life of these plastic covers has not been established when used exposed to the air or under slabs. Soil covers may be rolled out on the soil from foundation wall to wall. It is not necessary to form a complete seal over the soil, but more than 90 percent of the soil should be covered, and cracks should be limited to 1 inch. Removal of trash and debris and leveling of sharp dips and mounds in the soil will increase the life of the cover.

## SILLS AND BEAMS

Inspection and timely repair of sills and beams set on foundation walls, piers, or columns are important to the general maintenance of a structure. As in the case of uneven settlement of the foundation, severe damage can be done to the basic building by a reduction of the ability of the sill or beam to maintain upper components in their fixed position.

Sill and beam defects can lead to many lesser but troublesome and expensive repairs of wall and ceiling cracks and misaligned doors and windows. Wood sills and beams should be inspected periodically for rot and insect and rodent damage.

Sills and beams should be kept to correct grade by the use of slate or steel shims and mortar pointing. Reinforcing plates, extra tie-downs, or other means should be used to correct misalignment. Timbers exposed to ground moisture or severe weathering must be treated often enough to prevent deterioration, and sufficient ventilation assured to avoid rotting.

## POSTS AND COLUMNS

Periodic, thorough inspection should be made of all posts and columns in contact with the ground to detect deterioration. They should be treated with a preservative to resist decay and damage by termites. Posts and columns should be maintained plumb and in alignment. Inspection of posts should include a test for soundness, made by jabbing the post on all sides with an icepick or other sharp instrument; the amount of penetration indicates the soundness of the wood. In most soft woods, such as pine and fir, the pick should not penetrate more than $1/2$ inch; in hardwoods, such as gum and oak, penetration should not exceed $3/8$ inch. Columns are more difficult to inspect in finished buildings, but when there are indications that columns are out of plumb, the covering finish material should be removed and a thorough inspection made. Out-of-plumb or misaligned columns may be indicated by cracks in plaster or other finish, but the same defects may be caused by failure of other structural components. Repairs and/or replacement work should not be made until the true cause of defects is found.

If the foundation is not level because of uneven settling, the defect should be corrected before any attempt is made to plumb or align posts or columns. The floor above should then be shored with jacks or other devices, and the supporting members plumbed and realigned.

Posts or columns that show signs of failure caused by overloading should be surveyed by an engineer competent to recommend repairs or replacement in terms of overall structural soundness.

A wood post that is rotten at the ground level.

A concrete pier replaces the rotten end of the post.

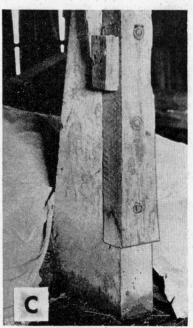

A precast stub post can also be used.

USDA Photos

# Index